GLOBETR

Travel

C000018018

NAMIBIA

WILLIE OLIVIER

NH
NEW
HOLLAND

★★★ Highly recommended
★★ Recommended
★ See if you can

Seventh edition published in 2010
by New Holland Publishers (UK) Ltd
London • Cape Town • Sydney • Auckland
10 9 8 7 6 5 4 3 2 1

website: www.newhollandpublishers.com

Garfield House, 86 Edgware Road
London W2 2EA, United Kingdom

80 McKenzie Street
Cape Town 8001, South Africa

Unit 1, 66 Gibbes Street,
Chatswood, NSW 2067, Australia

218 Lake Road, Northcote
Auckland, New Zealand

Distributed in the USA by
The Globe Pequot Press, Connecticut

ISBN 978 1 84773 681 9

This guidebook has been written by independent
authors and updaters. The information therein
represents their impartial opinion, and neither they
nor the publishers accept payment in return for
including in the book or writing more favourable
reviews of any of the establishments. Whilst every
effort has been made to ensure that this guidebook
is as accurate and up to date as possible, please be
aware that the facts quoted are subject to change,
particularly the price of food, transport and accommodation. The Publisher accepts no responsibility
or liability for any loss, injury or inconvenience
incurred by readers or travellers using this guide.

Publishing Manager: Thea Grobbelaar
DTP Cartographic Manager: Geneé Hart
Editors: Thea Grobbelaar, Nicky Steenkamp,
Sandie Vahl
Design and DTP: Nicole Bannister, Mandy Moss
Cartography: Reneé Spocter, Lauren Fick, Tanja
Spinola, Geneé Hart, Nicole Bannister
Reproduction by Hirt & Carter (Pty) Ltd, Cape Town
Printed and bound by Times Offset (M) Sdn. Bhd., Malaysia

Keep us Current
Information in travel guides is apt to change, which
is why we regularly update our guides. We'd be
grateful to receive feedback if you've noted some-
thing we should include in our updates. If you have
new information, please share it with us by writing
to the Publishing Manager, Globetrotter, at the
office nearest to you (addresses on this page). The
most significant contribution to each new edition
will receive a free copy of the updated guide.

Cover: *Sand dunes at Sossusvlei, Namib-Naukluft
National Park.*
Title page: *Quiver trees, southern Namibia.*

CONTENTS

1
Introducing
Namibia

Covering 824,269km² (318,250 sq miles), Namibia is a country of contrasting landscapes ranging from the world's oldest desert to rugged mountains, dense woodlands and lily-carpeted waterways. As a result, its fascinating plant and animal life is equally varied.

Windhoek, the capital, is situated among the rolling hills of the central highlands. Here, modern office blocks contrast with German colonial buildings and their pitched roofs. In the south, **Ai-Ais**, with its thermal springs, is tucked away among rugged mountainous terrain along the Fish River, while on the coast tranquil **Lüderitz** offers a retreat from the heat of the interior.

Namibia's premier holiday town **Swakopmund** is a pleasant coastal resort that can be used as a base for day excursions to the seal colony at **Cape Cross**, the **Namib Desert** with its stark gravel plains and **Sandwich Harbour**. The dune sea surrounding **Sossusvlei**, south of the Kuiseb River, can only be explored from **Sesriem**, on the edge of the desert; the rugged **Naukluft Mountains** are a hikers' paradise.

A four-wheel-drive is required for an expedition to the arid, extremely rugged **Kaokoland** in the northwest, but several tourist attractions in **Damaraland** and the southern part of the **Skeleton Coast National Park** are easily accessible by car.

At **Etosha National Park** with its shimmering pan, the large number of game is the attraction. **Mahango** and **Khaudum** game parks to the east also offer excellent game-viewing in a more wilderness atmosphere.

Opposite: *A gigantic sand dune at Sossusvlei.*

HIGHEST MOUNTAINS

Namibia's highest mountain, the **Brandberg**, does not form part of the escarpment chain, but rises abruptly from the surrounding gravel plains. Its peak, **Königstein**, with an altitude of 2579m (8461ft), was first ascended in 1918 by a party of three. The second highest peak in the country is the **Molkte-Blick** at 2483m (8146ft) in the Auas Mountains just south of Windhoek; third highest is the table-top 2351m (7713ft) **Gamsberg** on the edge of the Khomas Hochland.

Opposite: *A palm-fringed segment of the mighty Kunene River.*
Below: *Travellers in four-wheel-drive vehicles cross the desolate, hauntingly beautiful Marienfluss valley in Kaokoland.*

THE LAND
Plateau, Mountains and Plains

The topography of Namibia is characterized by a narrow coastal plain and a vast inland plateau that are separated by a rugged escarpment.

The **coastal plain** extends eastwards from the coast for between 80km (50 miles) and 120km (74.5 miles) to the escarpment. With an average annual rainfall of between about 10mm (0.4in) a year at the coast and 150mm (6in) in the Pro-Namib along the eastern edge of the desert, this region is an extremely arid tract of land.

The **escarpment** forms part of the Great Escarpment of southern Africa that extends from southern Angola in an arc to the Ukhahlamba Drakensberg and Mpumalanga Drakensberg. In Namibia it is characterized by a deeply eroded mountain chain stretching discontinuously from the Kunene River in the north to the Orange River in the south. The central highlands, a landscape of dissected rolling hills, are known as the **Khomas Hochland**.

East of the escarpment lies the **inland plateau**, an area of vast plains fringed by low mountains, scattered hills and *inselbergen* (island mountains). Further east, the landscape is dominated by low, rolling **Kalahari dunes**.

The **Caprivi**, in the far northeast of the country, is a region of rivers, narrow water channels and woodlands and is unlike any other part of Namibia.

Rivers

Although the landscape is crisscrossed by a number of rivers, they are often dry for several years as a result of the erratic rainfall. However, after heavy rains these **dry river courses** are turned into torrents, racing down to the sea where they discharge their muddy load. The underground water supply is recharged by these floods, providing a vital source of moisture for trees and animals during dry periods.

The only perennial rivers in Namibia are shared with its neighbours. In the south, the **Orange River** forms the border with South Africa for about 500km (311 miles), while the mighty **Kunene River** in the north forms part of Namibia's border with Angola for about 325km (202 miles). Winding through a primaeval landscape, the Kunene is characterized by thundering waterfalls, raging white-water rapids and tranquil streams. Further east, the **Kavango River** gushes over a series of cascades, the best known of which is the

Popa Falls, before continuing its journey to the famed Okavango Delta in Botswana.

Still further east, the **Kwando River** forms the boundary between Namibia, Angola and Zambia in the north, and after making its way through the Caprivi Strip, it serves as the border between Namibia and Botswana. Here it breaks up into a labyrinth of channels, islands and oxbow lakes to form the vast Linyanti Swamps. In the far northeast the **Zambezi River** serves as the frontier between Namibia and Zambia before plunging over the Victoria Falls in Zimbabwe.

Seas and Shores

Namibia's coastline of 1400km (2253 miles) is remark-ably even and there are only three major bays – Lüderitz, Sandwich and Walvis Bay. The coast is washed by the cold **Benguela Current**, which is partly responsible for the extremely arid conditions here and causes dense fog

---

RICHES FROM THE SEA

Despite the adverse climatic conditions created by the cold Atlantic Ocean, condi-tions are ideal for marine life, and the offshore waters of Namibia are among the richest fishing grounds in the world. **Demersal fishing** is the most important compo-nent of the fishing industry and concentrates on hake and monkfish. The bulk of pelagic catches (pilchards and juvenile horse mackerel) is processed into fish meal and oil, and pilchards are also canned. Kingklip, sole and tuna are other valuable marine resources.

and low clouds for up to 120 days a year. As a result, the coastal region is uninhabited, except for Oranjemund and Lüderitz in the south, and Walvis Bay, Swakopmund and Henties Bay further north. Moderate temperatures on the coast attract many holiday-makers escaping from the excessive midsummer heat in the interior.

Increasing attention is being paid to offshore diamond mining along Namibia's southern coast, while promising gas reserves have been discovered 150km (93 miles) off the coast of Oranjemund.

FACTS AND FIGURES

Highest point: Königstein (2579m; 8461ft).
Highest waterfall: Ruacana at 120m (394ft) high.
Highest sand dune: at Sossusvlei (325m; 1069ft).
Biggest dam: Hardap (25km²; 10 sq miles).
Largest meteorite: Hoba Meteorite (about 60 tonnes).
Deepest canyon: Fish River Canyon, (549m; 1801ft).

Climate

With an unpredictable annual **rainfall**, averaging 270mm (10.5in), and a very high evaporation rate, Namibia is largely an arid country, and the Namib Desert is one of the driest areas in the world. Except in the southwestern corner of the country, a winter-rainfall area, more than half of the precipitation is recorded between October and March, and usually occurs as violent **thunderstorms** during mid-afternoon or early evening.

Daytime **temperatures** in summer are usually high, peaking at over 40°C (104°F) in the south and north of the country. The central highlands are usually a bit cooler. Winter days are mild with low minimum temperatures.

COMPARATIVE CLIMATE CHART	WINDHOEK				ETOSHA				SWAKOPMUND			
	SUM	AUT	WIN	SPR	SUM	AUT	WIN	SPR	SUM	AUT	WIN	SPR
	JAN	APR	JULY	OCT	JAN	APR	JULY	OCT	JAN	APR	JULY	OCT
MAX TEMP. °C	36	29	25	35	33	31	26	35	21	20	18	6
MIN TEMP. °C	11	4	5	12	16	15	6	17	15	13	9	11
MAX TEMP. °F	96	84	78	95	92	87	78	94	69	67	64	62
MIN TEMP. °F	51	39	41	53	60	58	42	62	59	55	47	51
RAINFALL in	3	1.5	0	0.5	3	1	0	0	0	0	0	0
RAINFALL mm	78	38	1	11	75	26	0	7	1	1	0	0

Plant Life

As a result of the dramatic changes in climatic conditions from the coast to the northeast of the country, Namibia has a rich variety of plant life, ranging from hardy desert plants that can survive for years without rain to papyrus reeds and subtropical trees.

The fascination of Namibia's flora, however, does not lie in its diversity, but in the number of species that have adapted to survive in the inhospitable Namib Desert and the Pro-Namib. Best known is the **Welwitschia mirabilis**, a unique species that has commanded the attention of botanists worldwide since it was first recorded in 1859 (*see* page 68).

Some desert-adapted plants take in water through their leaves, while others have an extensive, shallow root system that enables them to absorb condensed fog.

A region of particular botanical interest is the winter-rainfall area of southwestern Namibia. The sandy gravel plains and rocky mountain slopes of this arid region are the habitat of a large number of the country's protected plants. Among these are the interesting **elephant's trunk**, which at a distance resembles a person, and a fascinating variety of **stone plants** (*Lithops*). Further inland towards the south the much-photographed **quiver tree**, or *kokerboom*, is found.

Nearly 60% of the land's vegetation is characterized by **savannas**, ranging from dwarf shrub in the south to camelthorn in the east and mopane in the northwest.

The dense **woodlands** in the northeast are in sharp contrast to the sparsely vegetated Namib Desert, while the **wetlands** of Eastern Caprivi are a complete surprise to the first-time visitor.

THE !NARA

This spiny curcubit is endemic to the Namib. It grows in sandy dune areas near river-beds as a dense, tangled mass with roots extending up to 15m (49ft) downward. The thorny melon-shaped fruits are an important source of food for the Topnaars, as well as for gemsbok, hyena, jackal and porcupine.

Opposite: *Sand dunes meet the Atlantic Ocean along the barren coast of the central Namib Dessert.*
Below: *The drought-resistant quiver tree.*

Wildlife

Namibia's wildlife ranges from highly specialized reptiles and beetles that are endemic to the Namib Desert to semi-aquatic and aquatic species that are restricted to the wetlands in north-eastern Namibia.

From the accounts of early travellers it is clear that Namibia was a wildlife paradise just over a century ago. Giraffe and even rhino

Above: *This desert-adapted gemsbok and its calf feed on moisture-laden plants to survive the dry periods.*

lived on the outer fringes of the desert, while large herds of antelope ventured deep into the Namib in search of grazing after good rains. Hunting, poaching and, above all, the restriction of migratory animals' movement by fences have reduced game numbers in many of the commercial farming regions. Game populations in communal conservancies in the northwest and northeast of the country have shown encouraging increases.

Fortunately, though, land has been set aside as game reserves, the best known being the **Etosha National Park**. It is a sanctuary for large herds of typical plains animals such as springbok, blue wildebeest and elephant, and it has the largest black rhino population in Africa.

In the northeast of the country **Khaudum Game Park**, a truly wild tract of land, is an important refuge for the endangered roan. Several antelope species such as red lechwe, waterbuck, reedbuck and sitatunga are restricted to the wetlands in the far northeast of Namibia where the prime attraction is the prolific birdlife.

Far too often the fascinating variety of lesser creatures are overlooked. Despite its hostile environment, the dunes and gravel plains of the **Namib-Naukluft Park** are the home to many endemic reptiles and beetles.

GEMSBOK

The gemsbok, relative of the Arabian oryx, is widely distributed throughout Namibia. It is an elegant antelope with magnificent straight horns and distinctive black and white facial marks. The horns of both sexes can reach a length of up to 1.2m (4ft). Well adapted to live in arid areas, the gemsbok can go for long periods without drinking water, and a complex network of blood vessels beneath the brain enables it to survive body temperatures of more than 45°C (113°F). This distinctive antelope features both on Namibia's coat of arms and on the 100 dollar banknote.

Conserving Namibia's Natural Heritage

Nearly 15% of the land enjoys conservation status. This is not only well above the percentage recommended by the IUCN, but also one of the highest in Africa.

Prior to independence, game parks were set aside without considering the people living in the area or any benefits to surrounding communities. However, Namibia's conservation authorities have since adopted a policy of **community-based natural resource management**. Communal conservancies have been established throughout the country, but mainly in the northwest and northeast. Control over the wildlife resources in these areas not only provides an incentive to the inhabitants to conserve the wildlife, but communities also benefit directly from natural resources and tourism.

Commercial farmers have also played an important role in conservation. In 1967 ownership of ordinary game on their property was transferred from the State to landowners. This provided an incentive to farmers to protect wildlife on their land and laid the foundation of Namibia's lucrative game-farming industry. There are numerous hunting farms throughout the country.

Non-governmental organizations (NGOs) helped to prevent the desert-dwelling animals of Damaraland and Kaokoland from being wiped out completely. The South African Nature Foundation (now WWF South Africa) and the South African-based Endangered Wildlife Trust gave financial support and publicity during the initial anti-poaching campaign. NGOs still active in the field include the Save the Rhino Trust and the Namibia Nature Foundation.

> **CONSERVATION AND THE CONSTITUTION**
>
> The Namibian Constitution guarantees the protection of the environment. **Article 95 (f)** provides for the promotion and maintenance of the welfare of the people by the State by adopting policies aimed at preserving the environment. **Article 95 (c)**, establishes an Ombudsman to investigate, amongst others, complaints related to the environment.

Below: *Well-nourished zebra in Etosha. The park is home to thousands of these strikingly marked animals.*

HISTORY IN BRIEF

There is evidence that people lived in Namibia for several thousand years during the **Stone Age**. What is amongst the oldest rock paintings discovered on the African continent were unearthed in a cave in the Hunsberg, north of the Orange River, between 1969 and 1982. The paintings were executed on flat rocks during the Middle Stone Age, and have been dated at between 27,000 and 25,000 years old.

Towards the end of the Stone Age **San hunter–gatherers**, also referred to as Bushmen, lived in scattered groups throughout the country. They were divided into three main groups, and although their hunting and gathering way of life imposed certain similarities, they were culturally distinct and spoke different languages.

The earliest record of the pastoral **Khoikhoi** who migrated to Namibia dates back about 2600 years. Initially they had only fat-tailed sheep with long legs, but acquired cattle later. They moved about constantly in search of grazing, and the remains of their settlements can be seen throughout Namibia, even along the Namib coast.

Bantu-speaking people also migrated into Namibia and settled in the north of the country, while the **Herero**, a nation of pastoralists, settled in central and eastern Namibia. Other groups, such as the **Oorlam Nama**, crossed the Orange River in the early 1800s, and the **Basters** came to Namibia from the Northern Cape in the late 1860s.

The first **European** to set foot along the Namib coast was the Portuguese explorer, Diego Cão, who landed at Cape Cross in 1486. Although whalers and other vessels used Walvis Bay and Sandwich Bay as harbours for more than two centuries, it was not until March 1878 that Britain annexed Walvis Bay and the area surrounding it.

Germany also began extending its influence in Africa, and on 24 April 1884 an

---

HISTORICAL CALENDAR

January 1486: Portuguese explorer Diego Cão erects *padrão* at Cape Cross.
12 March 1878: Britain annexes Walvis Bay enclave.
24 April 1884: German Protectorate declared over Lüderitz and surrounding area.
11 January 1904: Herero Uprising against German colonial rule. Subsequent extermination of Herero people ordered by Von Trotha.
9 July 1915: German troops surrender to armed forces of Union of South Africa during First World War.

17 December 1920: League of Nations entrusts South West Africa to Union of South Africa as a Mandate.
10 December 1959: Under apartheid rule resistance to forced removals in Windhoek results in 13 people being killed by South African Police.
26 August 1966: First clash between SWAPO soldiers and South African forces.
27 October 1966: United Nations General Assembly adopts Resolution 2145, terminating South Africa's Mandate over South West Africa.

21 July 1971: International Court of Justice rules SA's presence in Namibia illegal.
4 May 1978: SWAPO members killed in a South African attack on Cassinga in Angola.
29 September 1978: United Nations Security Council adopts Resolution 435 outlining a solution to the conflict.
17 June 1985: Five-party Transitional Government of National Unity inaugurated.
1 April 1989: United Nations Resolution 435 implemented.
21 March 1990: Namibia gains Independence.

area surrounding Lüderitz was declared a protectorate. Several other protectorates were also declared, and 'protection treaties' were signed with some of the tribes. By the end of 1884 German rule was firmly established.

However, the charismatic Chief of the Witbooi Nama, **Hendrik Witbooi**, refused to sign a 'protection treaty' and on 12 April 1893 the German *Schutztruppe* attacked his stronghold at Hoornkrans. Witbooi then adopted guerrilla warfare tactics and it was not until August 1894 that at last a treaty was signed between the Germans and the Witbooi after a nine-day battle in the Naukluft Mountains.

Namibians were systematically dispossessed of their land by the German colonial administration and, fearing the loss of more land, the Herero under **Maherero** rose against German rule on 11 January 1904. The uprising started while the Germans were engaged in quelling an uprising by the **Bondelswart Nama** in the south. The Herero were finally defeated at the Battle of the Waterberg on 11 August 1904 and forced to flee into the waterless wastes in the east of the territory, while others went into exile in Botswana, then called Bechuanaland. Tens of thousands of Herero died in the war and of hunger and thirst and the genocide that followed; about 9000 men, women and children were taken prisoner.

Other indigenous people also took up arms against the Germans. In the north, several hundred **Ndonga** warriors attacked Fort Namutoni on 28 January 1904, while in the south of the country **Hendrik Witbooi** declared war against the Germans on 3 October 1904, a struggle that was to last until the end of 1906.

Following the declaration of the **First World War** on 4 August 1914, the South African Union forces invaded the country, and on 9 July 1915 the German troops surrendered at Kilometre 500 near Otavi.

On 17 December 1920 the League of Nations confirmed South Africa's **Mandate** over South West Africa.

Above: *Jan Jonker Afrikaner, son of Jonker Afrikaner (see page 40), became chief of the Oorlam Nama in 1863.*

VON TROTHA'S EXTERMINATION ORDER

After the defeat of the **Herero** in August 1904, General Lothar Von Trotha, issued his notorious extermination order: 'The Herero nation must now leave the country … Within the German frontier every Herero, with or without a rifle, with or without cattle, will be shot.'

THE ODENDAAL PLAN

In keeping with South Africa's policy of **separate development**, a commission was appointed in 1962 under the chairmanship of F. H. Odendaal to devise a **homeland system** for Namibia. Eleven 'bantustans' for the indigenous people, covering 332,567km² (128,404 sq miles), or 40% of the country's surface, were proposed, and legislative assemblies were introduced for whites and coloureds. In 1968 representative authorities were established for the different population groups, but the International Court of Justice ruling of June 1971 made it clear that South Africa could not declare the 'bantustans' independent. Ethnic administrations were maintained in these 'homelands' until just before the implementation of Resolution 435.

Hardly any new administrative structures were adopted by the new rulers, and white settlement was expanded.

In the north, **Chief Mandume ya Ndemufayo** resisted territorial demands, while the **Bondelswart** took up arms in the south when the South African government interfered in the succession of their chiefs.

After the **Second World War**, the League of Nations was replaced by the United Nations (UN). South Africa's request to the UN to incorporate South West Africa as a fifth province was turned down; in turn South Africa refused to place the territory under UN guardianship. This heralded the start of a lengthy dispute.

The victory of the National Party in the 1948 election in South Africa meant the introduction of **apartheid** in both South Africa and the occupied territory.

The **South West Africa National Union (SWANU)** was founded in August 1959 as a protest to the continued illegal occupation of Namibia. The following month, SWANU was joined by the **Owamboland People's Organization (OPO)**, which was initially founded in Cape Town in 1958 as the Owamboland People's Congress to campaign for the abolition of the contract labour system. Enforced separate residential areas for different race groups was just one aspect of

the policy of apartheid. Resistance to the **forced removal** of people from the Old Location in Windhoek to the Katutura township in December 1959 was ruthlessly crushed by the South African Police. Eleven people were killed and more than 60 wounded in what has become known as Namibia's Sharpeville Massacre.

The alliance between SWANU and the OPO was shortlived, and on 19 April 1960 the OPO was transformed into a broad-based national movement, the **South West Africa People's Organization (SWAPO)**, with the aim of liberating the Namibian people from colonial oppression and exploitation. By now it had become apparent that liberation would not be achieved through UN intervention alone. In 1961 SWAPO decided to prepare for an **armed struggle**, and on 18 July 1966 issued a statement saying that it had no alternative but to take to arms to bring an end to South African rule.

From the 1950s, the international community, through the UN and the International Court of Justice (ICJ) exerted pressure on the South Africa government to withdraw from SWA/Namibia. In 1966 The UN terminated South Africa's Mandate over the territory, and a year later the 11-member **UN Council for South West Africa** was established. This body gave much non-military support to SWAPO, such as establishing education programmes, throughout the struggle. However, it was not until 1971 that South Africa's occupation of SWA/Namibia was declared illegal by the ICJ.

The first clash between SWAPO soldiers and the South African Police took place at Ongulumbashe in northern Namibia on 26 August 1966. South Africa co-operated closely with the Portuguese colonial authorities in Angola and SWAPO was, therefore, initially forced to operate from Zambia, more than 1000km (624 miles) from its most important support base.

Despite this drawback, not only did SWAPO succeed in mobilizing the masses in Namibia, but in the early 1970s it became clear that the South African Police could no longer cope with the situation and in April 1973 responsibility for counter-insurgency was taken over by the South African Defence Force (SADF). The conflict, mainly fought on Namibia's northern borders, was to continue until April 1989.

After Angolan independence in 1975 SWAPO based itself in that country. To complicate matters, Angola was fighting its own civil war between UNITA, backed by

Opposite: *Youngsters enjoy a game of soccer in Katutura, a township created under apartheid rule in the late 1950s. Jobs are scarce in Namibia, and many of these youths will unfortunately join the ranks of the unemployed.*

THE INTERNATIONAL COURT OF JUSTICE (ICJ)

South Africa's dispute with the UN over Namibia featured prominently in the ICJ over more than two decades. **1950:** ICJ says that South Africa is under no obligation to conclude a new trusteeship agreement with UN, but must accept the supervision of UN General Assembly. **1955 and 1956:** ICJ states that UN General Assembly is empowered to supervise South Africa's administration of SWA/Namibia. **1960:** Ethiopia and Liberia institute proceedings against South Africa at the ICJ, charging it with violating its Mandate. **1962:** South Africa challenges the jurisdiction of the Court over its affairs without success. **1966:** ICJ rejects claims by Ethiopia and Liberia. **1971:** South Africa's continued presence in Namibia is declared illegal by the ICJ.

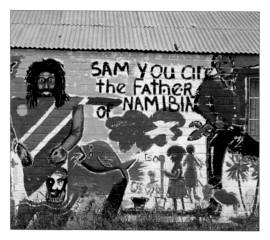

Above: *A colourful street mural in Katutura boldly expresses support for Sam Nujoma, Namibia's first president.*

CASSINGA

The liberation struggle entered a new phase when the SADF launched a pre-emptive strike against SWAPO's supposed head-quarters at Cassinga and other positions in southern Angola on 4 May 1978. Although reports of casualty figures are inconsistent, at least 600 SWAPO members were killed and several hundred were injured or captured. Most of those killed were innocent civilians. The tragedy attached to this event is commemorated in Namibia on 4 May.

South Africa, and the MPLA, supported by the Soviet Union and Cuba. The SADF invaded Angola in 1975.

Meanwhile, South Africa convened the internal parties in Namibia in Windhoek to draw up a constitution. This was the **Turnhalle Conference** of 1975, and the draft constitution that it produced in 1977, with the approval of South Africa, was rejected by the UN Security Council. South Africa went ahead with general elections in Namibia in 1978. SWAPO called for an election boycott, and the UN Security Council declared the whole process invalid. Nonetheless, the Democratic Turnhalle Alliance, who won the majority of the votes in the election, governed the country until 1983. A conference of internal parties, known as the **Multi-Party Conference** (MPC), was then convened in September 1983 and in May 1985 the MPC held talks with SWAPO in Lusaka. However, no agreement was reached and, on request of the internal parties, on 17 June the **Government of National Unity** was installed in Windhoek. Two days later the UN Security Council condemned the South African government's action towards determining the future political development of Namibia unilaterally and declared the action illegal.

Throughout this period when South Africa tried to install a pro-South Africa government in Windhoek diplomatic efforts for a negotiated settlement continued. In April 1978 South Africa accepted the proposals of the Western Contact Group for a settlement of the Namibian dispute. **Resolution 435** was adopted by the Security Council in September 1978. However, given the wide support SWAPO enjoyed, South Africa realized that the organization would win an internationally supervised election and so dragged its heels to buy more time in the hope of defeating SWAPO militarily.

To understand the processes that ultimately led to Namibian independence it is necessary to consider the security situation in southwestern Africa during the late 1980s. South Africa became increasingly involved in the conflict between the Angolan government (MPLA) and UNITA. If the latter was defeated, SWAPO would be in a position to open the battlefront eastwards by several hundred kilometres. The biggest land battle fought in this conflict, and, indeed, ever fought in Sub-Saharan Africa, took place in October 1987 at the Lomba River. The SADF forced the opposing forces to fall back west of the Cuito River. Ironically, the bloody battle that raged at **Cuito Cuanavale** and resulted in a stalemate proved to be the turning point in the search for a peaceful solution. The parties involved realized that peace could only be achieved through negotiations and not through the barrel of a gun, as an escalation of the war would demand a high price, economically and in human lives.

The ongoing **diplomatic negotiations** resulted in an agreement on a new initiative for Namibia's independence between South African Foreign Minister Pik Botha and the United States Assistant Secretary of State for African Affairs Chester Crocker in Geneva, March 1988. Several high-level meetings later the **trilateral agreement** was signed by Angola, Cuba and South Africa in New York, 22 December 1988. It made provision for the phased withdrawal of an estimated 50,000 Cuban troops from Angola and the implementation of Resolution 435 in Namibia under the supervision of the UN Secretary-General, assisted by UNTAG.

UNTAG

The United Nations Transition Assistance Group (UNTAG) was established in accordance with Resolution 435 to assist the Special Representative of the UN Secretary-General to supervise and control free and fair elections for a Constituent Assembly that would be responsible for drawing up a Constitution. The civilian component of UNTAG oversaw all aspects of the electoral process, while 500 police monitors supervised the proper maintenance of law and order. The military component of 4475 soldiers from 21 countries was responsible for monitoring the cessation of hostilities, and for supplying logistical support, communication and supplies for UNTAG's countrywide network.

Below: *UNTAG supervised the registration of voters for democratic elections in 1989.*

Above: *Queen Elizabeth II, seen here with President Nujoma, arrives for a state visit in 1991.*

Birth of a Nation

5 August 1988: Geneva Protocol for implementation of Resolution 435 set.
22 December 1988: Tripartite Agreement signed.
1 April 1989: Implementation of UN Resolution 435.
November 1989: Elections take place. SWAPO wins a 56.5% majority
9 February 1990: Constitution, drawn up by Constituent Assembly, adopted.
21 March 1990: Independence celebrations.
1 March 1994: Reintegration of Walvis Bay enclave and offshore islands.

Within hours of the implementation of **Resolution 435** on 1 April 1989 the process was nearly derailed when heavily armed SWAPO forces crossed from Angola into northern Namibia. South African troops were redeployed, and in the clashes that followed 305 SWAPO and 27 South African soldiers were killed. A historic meeting at Mount Etjo Safari Lodge on 8 and 9 April between representatives of Angola, Cuba and South Africa led to the **Mount Etjo Declaration** that brought the implementation of Resolution 435 back on track.

Another of UNTAG's tasks was to ensure the return of thousands of Namibians who went into exile during the liberation struggle. The **repatriation of refugees** got under way on 12 June 1989, and by the end of September of that year, 42,736 Namibians were re-settled, mainly from Angola and Zambia.

More than 97% of the 701,483 registered voters cast their ballots in the UNTAG-supervised election that took place between 7 and 11 November and was declared free and fair on 14 November. SWAPO won 56.5% of the vote, while the main opposition party, the Democratic Turnhalle Alliance (DTA), took 28.1% of the vote. Numerous overseas dignitaries, including Secretary-General of the UN, Javier Perez de Cuellar, were present at Independence Stadium on 21 March 1990 when the South Africa flag was lowered to be replace by the bright new Namibian flag and Sam Nujoma was inaugurated as the country's first democratically elected president.

In 1991 Namibia became a member of the Commonwealth. Diplomatic negotiations on the return of the **Walvis Bay** enclave and the offshore islands started soon after independence, and on 1 March 1994 the disputed territory was reintegrated into Namibia. Hifikepunye Pohamba was sworn in as Namibia's second president on 21 March 2005.

GOVERNMENT AND ECONOMY

Namibians elected their first **democratic government** in November 1989 under the supervision of UNTAG. SWAPO won 41 seats in the Constituent Assembly, while the DTA formed the official opposition with 21 seats, and five smaller parties claimed the other 10 places. A **Constitution** guaranteeing fundamental human rights and freedom was adopted on 9 February 1990 and is internationally viewed as both democratic and liberal. The powers of the State are divided between the Executive branch, the Legislative branch consisting of the 72-seat National Assembly and the National Council, and an independent judiciary.

The first years since independence have been characterized by political stability, and Namibia has often been hailed as a successful example of democracy in Africa.

To unify a nation that was torn apart by the liberation struggle, the government embarked on a policy of **national reconciliation**, while **affirmative action** has been implemented to ensure the advancement of the previously disadvantaged majority. To address inequalities between rich and poor, **sustained economic development** aimed at the eradication of poverty and the provision of better living standards is a national objective.

Since the liberation struggle was aimed at regaining the land dispossessed by the German and South African colonial administrations, the **redistribution of land** remains one of the most serious issue facing the government.

Infrastructure

The **road network** between the country's main towns is tarred, but minor gravel roads in rural areas, especially in the north, northwest and northeast, could be impassable after heavy rains.

Below: *Namibia's roads run as straight as arrows to far horizons.*

LINKING NAMIBIA TO SOUTHERN AFRICA

Prior to independence, Namibia's road system was oriented north-south, and the only major road links were with South Africa. However, since independence two major highway projects have been completed to improve Namibia's road links with other southern African countries. The **Trans-Kalahari Highway** not only links Namibia with Botswana, but also reduces the distance between Windhoek and Johannesburg by over 400km (248.5 miles). In the north-east of the country the **Trans-Caprivi Highway** provides a fully tarred road link between Namibia, Zambia, Zimbabwe and northern Botswana.

Rail services are provided by TransNamib, a government-owned corporation, and are predominantly freight-oriented. Passenger services are offered on all major routes. The major towns in the south, central and north-central regions, as well as Swakopmund and Walvis Bay on the coast and Gobabis in the east, are all served by the national rail network. Regular scheduled **bus services** between the country's major towns are provided by Intercape Mainliner.

Namibia has two **harbours**, Lüderitz in the south and Walvis Bay along the central Namibian coast.

The national **airline**, Air Namibia, operates regular international, regional and domestic passenger and freight services.

Agriculture

Namibia's relatively small formal agricultural sector is complemented by a large informal farming sector. Commercial agriculture is dominated by **livestock farming**, and beef accounts for about 80% of gross agricultural income. Cattle farming is centred in the eastern-central and central parts of the country, and the number of cattle fluctuates between 1.8 and 2.5 million. Namibia is renowned for its high-quality free-range beef, most of which is exported to South Africa, but prime beef is also

exported to the United Kingdom and other European Union countries. **Small-stock** farming is practised in the sparsely vegetated, dry south, and the sheep population, reared for meat and karakul pelts, numbers between 3 and 4 million. Other agricultural activities are **dryland crop production** of maize, **game farming** and the cultivation of crops such as cotton and vegetables under irrigation. Farming in the communal areas is **subsistence**-based and accounts for about 30% of the agricultural sector's contribution to the GDP. In the north the emphasis is on dry-land cultivation of **millet**, while in the east **cattle** farming dominates.

WALVIS BAY

Fishing

Prior to independence, Namibia's rich fishing resources were plundered by foreign fleets and nearly depleted. As a result of the implementation of stringent conservation measures and the declaration of a 200-nautical-mile Exclusive Economic Zone since then, however, the fishing resources have recovered remarkably.

Inshore pelagic fishing concentrates mainly on pilchards and anchovies, while large hake and horse mackerel stocks occur further **offshore**.

Lüderitz is the centre of the **rock-lobster** industry (see page 54). Due to over-exploitation and adverse marine conditions, annual catches decreased from 8600 tonnes in 1968 to only 130 tonnes in 1993–4, but stocks have still not recovered and the 2008 and 2009 quotas were set at 350 tonnes.

The contribution of **fishing** and **fish processing** to the GDP varies as the industry is affected by unfavourable marine environmental conditions. In 2008 fishing and fish processing on shore contributed 2,9% and 1.5% respectively to the GDP. The fishing industry is also one of the country's major employers.

Industry

Because of the relatively small domestic market and reliance on imports from South Africa, Namibia's manufacturing industry is poorly developed and its

Above: *Fishermen on a pilchard trawler at Walvis Bay, centre of Namibia's fishing industry.*
Opposite: *A herdsman watches over a herd of goats. Small stock such as sheep and goats are reared mainly in the arid south.*

MINING

Namibia's mining industry is the fifth largest in Africa and approximately 30 different **minerals** and **metals**, as well as **precious** and **semiprecious stones**, are mined in the country. Between 2004 and 2008 mining accounted for between 9,7% and 15.9% of Namibia's GDP. The most important mining products of the country are diamonds, uranium, copper, lead and zinc, while gold, silver, salt and a variety of semiprecious stones are also mined here.

MAJOR EXPORTS

- Diamonds
- Base metals, precious metals and minerals
- Food and live animals
- Manufactured products (e.g. fish, beer and soft drinks)

contribution to the GDP is a mere 10%. The most important activities are **meat** and **fish processing**, as well as the manufacturing and assembling of **mining, construction** and **agricultural equipment**. The informal manufacturing sector is also undeveloped, but has considerable potential. Special incentives have been created to encourage investment in the manufacturing section of the economy.

Energy

Nampower, the national power utility, is responsible for bulk **electricity supply** throughout Namibia. Since the capacity of the Ruacana hydro-electric plant on the Kunene River is insufficient to meet the country's growing demand for electricity, Nampower's grid is linked to the South African power utility, Eskom. This allows power to be exported or imported to and from South Africa. Prior to independence, the central and southern parts of the country had a well-developed electricity network, but the electrification of rural areas countrywide had been neglected. Many rural communities in the northern, eastern and southern regions have, however, been linked to the national electricity grid since independence. Plans to build a second hydro-electric scheme at Epupa, 120km (74.5 miles) downstream of Ruacana, were announced in 1990. The project has failed to get off the ground, but there has been talk of going ahead with it at a site in the Baynes Mountains, downstream of Epupa.

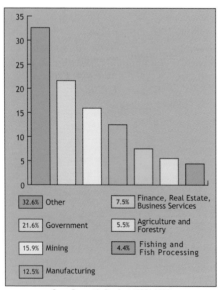

32.6%	Other	7.5%	Finance, Real Estate, Business Services
21.6%	Government	5.5%	Agriculture and Forestry
15.9%	Mining	4.4%	Fishing and Fish Processing
12.5%	Manufacturing		

Gross Domestic Product (GDP) 2008

Social Services

Nearly 15% of the national budget is allocated annually to **health** and **social services**. Since independence the emphasis of the government's health policy has shifted from curative care to primary-health community-based health care.

Namibia has one of the best doctor : patient ratios in Africa, with one doctor for every 3650 persons, while the ratio of three hospital beds per 1000 people is also one of the highest in the continent.

THE PEOPLE

Namibia is a sparsely populated country with an average **population density** of 2 people per km² (0.4 sq miles). Population densities range from one person per 6km² (2.3 sq miles) in the arid south to nearly 12 persons per km² (0.4 sq miles) in the north. Around 60% of the country's 2 million people still live in rural areas.

Religion

Namibia is a non-secular state, with freedom of religion guaranteed in the Constitution. About 90% of the people are **Christians**, while small **Jewish** and **Moslem** communities are centred in Windhoek.

About 50% of the Christian population belongs to the three **Lutheran** churches. The **Dutch Reformed** Church ministers to Afrikaans-speaking communities. Other major denominations are the **Roman Catholic** Church, the **Anglican** Church and the **Methodist** Church.

During the liberation struggle, the **Council of Churches in Namibia** (CCN), formed in 1978 to promote ecumenical spirit among churches, played a leading role in highlighting the plight of the voiceless masses.

Language

On independence **English** became the official language of the country, but **Afrikaans** is still the *lingua franca* in large parts of Namibia, except in Caprivi where English is spoken. **German** is widely spoken in towns such as Lüderitz and Swakopmund, as well as in numerous businesses throughout Namibia.

The most commonly spoken indigenous languages are **Kwanyama**, a dialect of Oshiwambo, and **Ndonga**. Others languages spoken include **Herero**, **Damara/Nama**, four dialects of **Kavango**

TRADITIONAL RELIGION

Although 90% of Namibia's people are Christian, traditional religious beliefs and Christianity are still practised side by side, especially in the rural areas. **Ancestor cult** links the present social order with the living dead or ancestors. Nowhere is this better illustrated than at the annual Herero Day celebrations when the **Herero** pay tribute to their forefathers. The processions are preceded by various rituals and communication with deceased leaders.

Traditional religious beliefs are still fairly common among the **Himba** and **San** who have not been exposed to Christianity to the same extent as have people from other cultures.

Below: *Preparing for Sunday worship in a charming little church in the east of the Kavango Region.*

(Kwangali, Mbukushu, Gciriku and Mbunza), **Lozi**, **Setswana** and **San**.

Traditional Cultures

Namibia's people have mostly assimilated the Western culture imposed on them by the colonists, so there is little to be seen of traditional dress and culture, except in the remote parts of Namibia.

Above: *The traditional dress of Herero women is derived from the fashions worn by 19th-century missionary wives.*
Opposite: *The distinctive face of the Topnaars of the Lower Kuiseb River valley.*

LANGUAGES

English is the official language of Namibia, but is the home language of only 0.9% of the population. Languages (home or first) spoken by Namibian people are:
- Owambo languages 50.6%
- Damara/Nama 12.5%
- Kavango languages 9.7%
- Afrikaans 9.5%
- Herero 8.0%
- Caprivi languages 4.7%
- San languages 1.9%
- English 0.9%
- Tswana 0.4%
- Other languages (including German) 1.0%

Owambo

The **Owambo** people constitute approximately half of the Namibian population and are divided into eight groups. More than 50% of the Owambo people are members of the two largest groups, the Kwanyama and the Ndonga.

San

During the early 1900s small groups of San **hunter-gatherers** were widely distributed throughout Namibia. Within less than a century, those who escaped extermination were either assimilated by other cultural groups or dispossessed of their hunting and gathering grounds.

Their demise was accelerated when farmers established themselves in their traditional areas, and in the late 1970s many of the men were recruited as soldiers by the South African Defence Force (SADF). When the SADF withdrew from Namibia, they were left destitute and many San, especially the younger generation, no longer knew the skills of hunting and gathering.

Today there are no San communities in Namibia living exclusively from hunting and gathering. Likewise, the skin aprons and other traditional clothing have almost completely been replaced by Western garb. The largest concentrations of San people live in the former **Bushmanland** and in **Western Caprivi**.

Herero

The Herero-speaking people consist of the Himba and the Tjimba of northwestern Namibia, the Herero of central and eastern Namibia and the Mbanderu in the east. Their economy, customs and religion are centred around **cattle**, while **ancestor worship** plays an important role in their culture and beliefs.

Colourful ceremonies are held each year to pay respect to their forefathers. At Okahandja, the 'Red Flag' Herero commemorate Maherero Day in August, and the Mbanderu or 'Green Flag' Herero honour their ancestral leader in June (*see* page 40). The 'White Flag' Herero pay homage to Chief Zeraua at Omaruru in October.

Himba

The Himba of northwestern Namibia, who are Herero people that chose to stay in Kaokoland when most of the Herero migrated to central Namibia during the 18th century, are the most exclusively **pastoral** of all Bantu-language speakers in southwestern Africa. Because of the isolation in which they live, even by today's standards, the Himba have until quite recently been little affected by Western influences.

The economic activity of the Himba centres around subsistence pastoralism, and prior to the devastating drought of the early 1980s they were one of the most wealthiest cattle-herder nations in Africa. They are semi-nomadic, moving constantly in search of grazing and water for their livestock.

While most Himba men have adopted some form of Western dress, women still wear their **traditional dress** of leather aprons, thongs and headdresses.

Topnaars

The Topnaars are one of nine Nama tribes, and are among the earliest inhabitants of Namibia. They live mainly in the **Lower Kuiseb River valley** and **Walvis Bay** areas,

A TRADITIONAL WAY OF LIFE

A striking feature of the **Himba** women is the paste of ochre powder and animal fat that they apply to their skin and hair both as protection from the harsh sun and as a cosmetic. Himba settlements are distinguished from those of the Herero by their circular and conical houses with a slight tunnel entrance; Herero houses are usually square or oblong with upright walls and roofs. An important feature of any Himba settlement is the sacred fire, which plays a central role in ritual and social functions at which the male head of the family officiates. Responsibility for the holy fire, however, rests with his mother, and after her death, his senior wife.

EKIPA BUTTONS

Ekipa buttons carved from ivory were worn by **Owambo** women at the turn of the century as a symbol of wealth, and jewellers have reintroduced this ancient craft by using legal ivory. These pieces of jewellery are usually round or oval, with a diameter of 5cm (2in), and are sometimes boat-shaped.

The ekipa had different patterns carved into them and were then rubbed with a powder derived from teak wood or the juice of aloes to accentuate the patterns. A leather thong was threaded through a hole drilled on the flat underside of the button, and it was then worn around the neck, the upper arm or at the back of the head; alternatively, the ekipa was fastened on to a wide belt.

while a small community also lives at **Sesfontein**, about 500km (311 miles) north of these two areas. The Topnaars of the Lower Kuiseb live in 12 semi-permanent settlements along the northern banks of the Kuiseb River, and the community totals about 400 people.

Traditionally **pastoralists**, they used to supplement their diet by hunting, collecting seafood and gathering. Although the **!nara** (*see* page 9) is no longer their staple diet, this unusual plant still plays an important role in their economy, culture and diet. !Nara fields are owned by families and the property rights are hereditary. The kernels of the fruit are an important source of income.

Basters

The Basters of Namibia are a people of mixed stock, the descendants of the early white settlers at the Cape and Khoikhoi women. They settled in the vicinity of the hot springs at **Rehoboth** in 1870, having crossed the Orange River two years earlier to avoid confrontation with white *trekboers* who were encroaching on their territory.

Unlike in South Africa where the word 'baster' has a pejorative meaning, the Basters of the Rehoboth Gebiet, 90km (56 miles) south of Windhoek, are proud of their name. The main language spoken is **Afrikaans**. They are economically active in the building trade, as well as in commerce and industry, while small-stock farming is practised in the rural areas of the Rehoboth Gebiet.

Right: *Splendid catches are recorded on the Namibian coast.*

Sport and Recreation

Namibia's coast is renowned for its excellent **angling** conditions, and in summer thousands of people flock to the coastal resorts here. The **hunting** of game to make *biltong* is a popular pastime during the winter months.

Football has the largest following in Namibia and is undoubtedly the national sport. During the season, from February to November, league and friendly matches are played every weekend, often on fields without any facilities.

Rugby, golf, tennis, as well as cricket, are also popular.

Athletics has attracted more attention after the excellent performance of Namibian sprinter Frank Fredericks in the 100m and 200m at the 1992 and 1996 Olympic Games and the silver medal won by Luketz Swartbooi for the marathon at the 1993 World Games.

Food and Drink

Eateries in Namibia offer a variety of continental, German and South African fare and a truly Namibian culinary identity has developed over the past two decades.

Many restaurants include **game** on their menus. Kudu, springbok and gemsbok dishes are the most popular, while zebra, ostrich and other game specialities are occasionally offered. As Namibia is a major beef-producing country, **beef** steaks and dishes feature prominently on menus. A variety of **processed meats** and **sausages**, prepared in the traditional German style, are often served at cold buffets.

The traditional South African **braaivleis**, or barbecue, is a favourite for outdoor entertainment, while fresh linefish like steenbras and kabeljou, as well as oysters from Lüderitz and Swakopmund, are popular **seafood** fare.

In this dry and hot country **beer** is the national drink. It is generally light and refreshing and brewed in the traditional German way as decreed by Duke Wilhelm of Bavaria in 1516. Also popular is a wide range of imported **German liqueurs** and *schnapps*, and a good selection of **South African wines** are available.

FOOD FOR THOUGHT

Biltong: spiced dried meat of Dutch origin.

Braaivleis: grilled (or barbecued) meal made outdoors.

Brötchen: German breadroll

Galjoen: popular firm-fleshed line fish.

Landjäger: German smoked beef and pork sausage.

Omajova: mushroom that grows on termite hills after the summer rains.

Schwarzwälder Torte: German Black Forest cake.

Sosatie: a South African version of the kebab.

Truffles: nut-flavoured fungus that grows underground in the Kalahari sands after rains.

2
Windhoek and Surrounds

Central Namibia is characterized by rolling hills which are deeply incised by numerous usually dry river courses that drain the inland plateau. Here Windhoek, Namibia's capital city, is sheltered by the Auas Mountains to the south and the Eros Mountains in the east. Situated at an altitude of between 1500m (4921ft) and 2000m (6562ft), the **Khomas Hochland** west of Windhoek derives its name from the Nama word 'Khomas', meaning hilly or mountainous terrain, and the German word 'Hochland', which refers to the plateau.

Farmers in the region surrounding Windhoek concentrate their efforts on beef production, while south of **Rehoboth** the wide open plains are ideally suited to small-stock farming.

For many visitors, **Windhoek** with its vibrant variety of African and Western cultures and old colonial German buildings is the starting point for a tour of well-known attractions in the country. Although many of the places of interest in central Namibia are easy day visits from the capital, they are also convenient as stopovers for travellers en route to destinations further afield.

Hardap Dam, some 260km (162 miles) south of Windhoek, offers excellent opportunities for game-viewing, bird-watching, freshwater angling and water sports, and is a popular place to stop on a trip to the south. To the north of the capital, the resort of **Gross Barmen**, centred on a thermal spring, offers a pleasant break for travellers, while at **Okahandja** the colourful annual processions are a main attraction.

CLIMATE

Summers here are **hot** with daily highs of over 28°C (82°F) between October and February; evenings are usually cooler. **Winter** days are **milder**, with maximum and minimum means of 20°C (69°F) and 6°C (43°F) in July, but early mornings and evenings are crisp with occasional **frost**.

Windhoek's average annual **rainfall** is 365mm (142in); Mariental has a mean of 210mm (8in). Two-thirds falls between January and March, generally as violent **thunderstorms**.

Opposite: *Looking down Independence Avenue.*

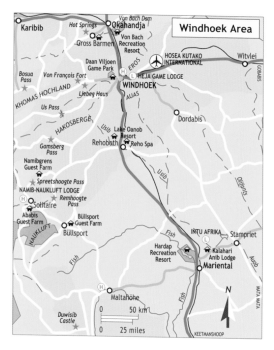

Windhoek Area

WINDHOEK

Although Windhoek has an estimated population of approximately 240,000, you are likely to get the initial impression that the city is even smaller. This is because Windhoek lies in a wide valley with its suburbs tucked away in the surrounding hills. It is on account of this undulating terrain that the airport is located 45km (28 miles) from the city centre.

City Walks **

The **National Botanic Garden of Namibia** on the slopes of the ridge between the city centre and Klein Windhoek provides an ideal introduction to the flora of Namibia's highlands and also has an interesting collection of succulents. The natural vegetation is virtually undisturbed and the Windhoek aloes (the city's emblem) are a delight in April and May when they flower. The Garden is open from 08:00 to 17:00 weekdays and on the first weekend of every month. The entrance is at 8 Orban Street.

Towards the end of the 19th century, when the Germans settled here, the area with its springs was already popular with the Oorlam Afrikaners and the Herero. Stone Age tools about 5000 years old and fossilized elephant bones excavated in **Zoo Park**, a tranquil oasis in the centre of Windhoek, are evidence that the springs have attracted man and beast for millennia.

Walk down **Independence Avenue**, Windhoek's main thoroughfare, and you will notice the colonial German architectural influence. Three restored build-

DON'T MISS

*** Herero and Mbanderu Processions: observe these colourful annual events in Okahandja.
*** Khomas Hochland: drive down one of the dramatic passes.
** Windhoek city walks: admire German colonial architecture and enjoy a bird's-eye view of the city.
** Namibian Craft Centre: purchase a variety of authentic Namibian souvenirs.
* Gross Barmen: relax in the therapeutic thermal spring.

ings in the street can be admired from under the palm trees in Zoo Park across the road. Here a plaque points out **Erkrath Building** (1913), **Gathemann House** (1913) with its steep roof and **Hotel Kronprinz** (1902).

Also in Independence Avenue, the **clock tower** at the intersection with Post Street Mall is an obvious landmark. It resembles the corner tower of the Deutsch-Afrika-Bank, built in 1908 but later demolished.

From Monday to Saturday the **Post Street Mall** bustles with shoppers at the morning street market where handicrafts ranging from wooden toys and rag dolls to Kavango woodcarvings and Zimbabwean malachite jewellery can be purchased.

Further down the Mall you can closely inspect the 31 **Gibeon Meteorites** on display. Although they could be mistaken for ordinary rocks, one has been sawn through to confirm their metal content. To date more than 77 meteorites have been recovered from the vicinity of Gibeon, south of Mariental.

The **Windhoek Information and Publicity (WIP)** bureau is in Post Street Mall.

KATUTURA

In 1959 the city's black people were forcibly moved to Katutura, a Herero word that means 'we have no dwelling place'. Thirteen people were killed in clashes with the Police on 10 December 1959, an event commemorated as **Human Rights Day**.

Housing in Katutura ranges from luxury homes to squatter settlements.

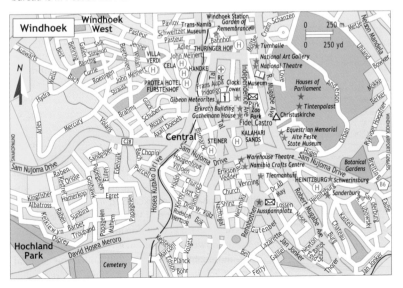

THE STATE MUSEUM

The State Museum in Robert Mugabe Avenue is housed in two buildings. If you are interested in archaeology and the cultural backgrounds of the indigenous people of Namibia, visit the **Owela Museum Display Centre** which is situated between Robert Mugabe Avenue and Lüderitz Street.

It is not only the design of the **Alte Feste**, which houses the other section of the State Museum, that is of interest; a variety of displays focus on the country's national symbols, the independence process, local household furniture, and implements used by the first European settlers.

Below: *The tall-steepled Christuskirche viewed from the imposing Tintenpalast.*

Guarding over the city centre is the almost fairytale **Christuskirche** (Church of Christ) in Robert Mugabe Avenue, completed in 1910 by the German Evangelical community as a monument to peace. Behind it is the **Tintenpalast** (Ink Palace), which was built in 1913 and now houses the Namibian Parliament, with its shady lawns and attractive gardens

Built in 1890, the **Alte Fest** (old fort) is Windhoek's oldest surviving building. The **Equestrian Memorial** was unveiled in 1912 in memory of the Germans killed in the Nama/Herero wars of 1903–07. It was moved in 2009 to make way for a Liberation Stuggle Museum and will be re-erected next to the fort.

Other imposing German colonial buildings include the **officers' house** (now the Bank of Namibia training centre), and the **old school building**, which now houses the museum staff, with its quaint tower.

Windhoek's Castles

Perched on the hill that separates Klein Windhoek and Windhoek are three 'castles'. They were designed by Willi Sander who was also responsible for Duwisib Castle (*see*

page 39). **Schwerinsburg**, initially a watchtower and a small tavern, was completed in 1914, followed by **Heinitzburg** and **Sanderburg** (built for Sander himself) in 1917. Heinitzburg is an upmarket hotel; the other two 'castles' are privately owned.

Shopping **

Ostrich-skin and buffalo-hide **leather goods** and **Swakara** jackets are very good buys here as prices are reasonable compared to what you would pay in Europe. Shops that sell Nakara garments and leather goods are Seelenbinder and Swakara in Independence Avenue and Leathers Unlimited in Post Street Mall.

Much of the locally handcrafted **jewellery** is inspired by the diverse Namibian landscape. Although most of the jewellers were trained in Germany, their work has an African flair and is not as heavy-looking as that produced in Europe. Agates, semiprecious stones from northwestern Namibia, as well as tourmalines and diamonds, are incorporated in the silver and gold pieces. Shops to visit in Independence Avenue are Adrian and Meyer, Canto Jewellers in Jack Levinson Arcade and Herrle & Herma Jewellers.

Gemstone collectors can browse through a number of shops – Rocks and Gems, Independence Avenue, and The House of Gems, Werner List Street. Take care, though, when buying gemstones from curio shops as you could be buying a stone imported from South America.

The **Namibia Crafts Centre** in the Old Brewery Building in Tal Street is the place to buy souvenirs such as African-style clothing and colourfully embroidered household goods, including cushion covers and tablecloths. Basketry, wood and stone carvings can also be bought at the Post Street Mall market and at the

Above: *Herero women display handcrafted dolls dressed in traditional garb.*

THEATRES AND ART GALLERIES

• The **Warehouse Theatre**, in the old brewery in Tal Street, usually stages music performances and one-man shows.
• The **National Theatre of Namibia**, situated on the corner of John Meinert Street and Robert Mugabe Avenue, presents occasional cultural performances.
• The **College of Arts** in Fidel Castro Street has occasional music, ballet and modern dance performances.
• The **National Art Gallery of Namibia**, on the corner of Robert Mugabe Avenue and John Meinert Street, has a permanent exhibition of Namibian art.
• **Commercial galleries** selling local art include Kendzia Framing, Volans Street, and the Omba Gallery in the Old Breweries Building.

bus terminus on the corner of Fidel Castro Street and Independence Avenue. The Bushman Art curio shop in Independence Avenue has an interesting variety of authentic Namibian **curios** and **karakul rugs**, while African Curiotique and Rogl Souvenirs in Independence Avenue are also well worth a visit.

Above: *The green and pleasant landscape of the Daan Viljoen Game Park.*
Opposite: *Liebig Haus, a relic of Namibia's German colonial past.*

GAME-VIEWING AND BIRD-WATCHING

Visitors will find a visit to the **Daan Viljoen Game Park** rewarding as the wildlife can be observed at fairly close range. Resident antelope include blue wildebeest, red hartebeest, kudu, eland, gemsbok, impala and spring-bok, and other mammals you may see are Hartmann's mountain zebra, warthog, chacma baboon, klipspringer, steenbok and rock dassies.

With about 260 bird species in the park, bird-watching can be rewarding too, and in summer you could spot up to 60 species. Look out for Monteiro's horn-bill, rockrunner and white-tailed shrike.

Daan Viljoen Game Park

This small game park, about 20km (12 miles) west of Windhoek along a tarred road, offers alternative overnight accommodation for visitors to the city. Situated pic-turesquely on the banks of the Augeigas Dam, the accom-modation units and facilities are being redeveloped by a private investor. The park is popular with Windhoekers over weekends and on public holidays but on one of the walks you can enjoy peace and tranquillity.

There is a short circular game-viewing drive through the Daan Viljoen Game Park, but perhaps the best way to familiarize yourself with the range of flora and fauna typical of the undulating hills of the Khomas Hochland is to set out on foot and tackle either the 3km (2-mile) **Wag 'n Bietjie Trail** or alternatively the more strenuous 9km (5.5-mile) **Rooibos Trail**. The focal point of the first trail is the Stengel Dam where you could spot game, while magnificent views over the Khomas Hochland are a highlight of the longer route. The more fit may prefer to tackle the **Sweet Thorn Hiking Trail**, a two-day route over about 32km (20 miles).

Among the facilities at Daan Viljoen are an inviting swimming pool and a good restaurant which serves breakfast, buffet lunches and dinners, and there are also a number of picnic and campfire places for day visitors. Contact Namibia Wildlife Resorts in Windhoek for reservations and information.

Khomas Hochland

West of Windhoek the hilly highland plateau of central Namibia is traversed by three gravel-surface routes which lead down the **Gamsberg**, **Us** or **Bosua** passes to the Namib Desert. A day drive from the capital to the top of one of these passes and back will reward you with views of the seemingly never-ending rolling hills which abruptly drop away to the vast plains of the desert.

Of particular interest on the route via Daan Viljoen Game Park to the top of the Bosua Pass are Liebig Haus, about 42km (26 miles) west of Windhoek, and further on the ruins of Von François Fort.

Liebig Haus was built in 1912–13 and, although now rather ramshackle, it still creates an imposing scene besides looking rather incongruous. Features like the steeply pitched roof, which was designed to allow snow to slide off, and the solarium indicate that the house was typical of those built in Germany at the time.

Just as fascinating is the **Von François Fort** which was built in 1890 by Major Curt von François when he moved his headquarters from Tsoabis to Windhoek. Subsequently German soldiers guilty of drunkenness were sent to this outpost, hence it was given the name *Trockenposten* (meaning 'dry post').

HORSE TRAILS

You can explore the Khomas Hochland and Namib Desert on horseback. **ReitSafari** offers a variety of horse trails throughout Namibia, including a nine-day 400km trail that leads from the Khomas Hochland down the escarpment and through the Namib to the coast. Trails are also conducted in Damaraland, Bushmanland, the southern Namib and the Sperrgebiet. The trails are fully catered.

Above: *The attractive Rehoboth Museum.*

Although there are a number of guest farms that are closer to Windhoek, **Namibgrens Guest Farm** near the summit of the **Spreetshoogte Pass** is reached after a pleasant drive through the Khomas Hochland. Views of the Namib from the top of the pass are spectacular.

Rehoboth

The therapeutic thermal spring and an interesting museum are the attractions of this often bypassed town.

Less than an hour's drive (80km; 50 miles) south of Windhoek, you will pass the turnoff to Rehoboth's water storage dam, the **Oanob Dam**, shortly before entering the town. Construction was completed in 1990, and the reservoir has a storage capacity of 35 million m³ (1236 million cu ft). **Lake Oanob Resort** has fully equipped self-catering chalets, a restaurant, bars, camping sites and picnic spots for day visitors. The resort's marina has a swimming pool and offers a variety of water sports – boating, canoeing, water-skiing and aqua-biking.

The **Basters**, a mixed race of Khoikhoi and Dutch people who originated in South Africa, settled around the hot-water spring here in 1870. The history of the Baster people is well illustrated in the **Rehoboth**

Museum which was once the home of the town's first postmaster. Other displays feature aspects of the life of the former San inhabitants of the area. By prior arrangement you can also visit an archaeological excavation of an **open-air burial site** of Late Iron Age people close by.

MARIENTAL AND SURROUNDS

Just north of Mariental a signpost indicates the turnoff to **Stampriet**, 52km (32 miles) on along a tarred road. The strong artesian waters which were discovered here in 1910 irrigate a variety of crops, and the area is renowned for its watermelons, sweet melons and grapes.

From here a gravel-surface road follows the course of the Auob River, ending abruptly at **Mata Mata** on the South African border. This entrance gate to the Kgalagadi Transfrontier Park was reopened in October 2007, following its closure at Namibia's independence. Travellers must stay two or more nights at any of the official overnight facilities in the park. The gate is open daily from 08:00–16:30.

Situated about halfway between Windhoek and Keetmanshoop is **Mariental**, the administrative hub of the Hardap region and an important agricultural centre. It has little to offer tourists, but worthy of mention are the nearby Hardap Recreation Resort and the **Kalahari Anib Lodge**, which offers guided drives and walks through the rolling dunes of the Kalahari.

Hardap Recreation Resort

The focal point of the resort is the 25km² (10-sq-mile) reservoir of the **Hardap Dam**, Namibia's largest. It was completed in 1962 by constructing a wall 865m (2838ft) in length between two outcrops along the course of the Fish River. The spectacular Fish River Canyon is further downstream.

Below: *A devout member of Namibia's 50,000-strong Afrikaans-speaking Baster community. Her forefathers arrived from the Cape in 1870 to settle in and around Rehoboth, to the south of Windhoek.*

The dam supplies water to Mariental and the 40-odd smallholdings of the Hardap Scheme where a variety of crops are cultivated under irrigation.

The large reservoir is especially popular with watersport enthusiasts, and at weekends large numbers of people flock here to enjoy waterskiing, sailing and windsurfing. Freshwater angling is another popular pastime, and there are several fishing spots with facilities for day visitors along the northern shore of the dam, which is stocked with eight species of freshwater fish.

The rest camp on the cliffs offers a choice of accommodation ranging from bungalows to dormitories and two-bed rooms, as well as camping and caravan sites. A special feature of the resort is the restaurant with its commanding view over the dam where visitors are served breakfast, buffet lunches and dinners, while the swimming pool is much appreciated on hot summer days. Contact Namibia Wildlife Resorts in Windhoek for reservations and information.

Game which can be found in the not often visited **Hardap Game Reserve** in the southwestern section of the resort includes gemsbok, springbok, kudu, red

hartebeest, steenbok and Hartmann's mountain zebra. There is also a possibility that you may encounter black rhino of Namibia's western subspecies. Hikers in particular should watch out for this potentially dangerous animal when undertaking the 9km (5.5-mile) or 15km (9-mile) self-guided circular trail.

Maltahöhe and Duwisib Castle

Travel westwards from Mariental and you will reach the small settlement of **Maltahöhe** after about an hour's drive along a tarred road. Situated on the edge of the Schwarzrand plateau, the town lies at the centre of an important karakul farming district. It is within easy reach of attractions such as Duwisib Castle, as well as Sesriem and Sossusvlei, and is a convenient stopover between Lüderitz and Swakopmund. The **Maltahöhe Hotel**, with its quaint bar, has been a watering hole for travellers since 1907.

The stone fortress **Duwisib**, 70km (43 miles) south of Maltahöhe, seems altogether misplaced in its almost desolate setting. It is constructed from red-brown stone quarried close by and blends in extremely well with the surrounding hills, so well that you usually notice it only when you reach the signpost for the turnoff. There is a camp site with ablutions and campfire places under shady camel thorn trees in the grounds below the castle. Contact Namibia Wildlife Resorts in Windhoek for reservations and information.

Above: *The romantic German colonial fortress-like former home of Captain Von Wolf, Duwisib Castle, has been restored.*
Opposite: *The limpid waters of Hardap Dam, northwest of Mariental, are a popular venue for anglers and water-sport enthusiasts.*

HERERO FOREFATHERS

Hosea Kutako (1872–1970): Herero chief, strongly opposed to South African occupation, was the first to petition the UN (in 1946). Committed to unity among Namibia's people, he chose to be buried near Jonker Afrikaner (c1785–1861), enemy of the Herero people, rather than in the cemetery where Tjamuaha, Maherero and Samuel Maherero were laid to rest.

Clemens Kapuuo (1923–78): succeeded Kutako, and became first President of Democratic Turnhalle Alliance (DTA) in 1977. He was assassinated in Windhoek, 27 March 1978.

MURDER HILL

A small outcrop along the B2 bypassing Okahandja serves as a reminder of the numerous battles fought between the Oorlam Afrikaners and their allies and the Herero. The vast herds of cattle owned by the Herero were irresistible to the Afrikaners who conducted numerous raids against the Herero despite peace agreements of 1842 and 1870. About 700 followers of the Herero Chief, Kahitjene, were killed in the battle at this outcrop in August 1850. It later became known as Moordkoppie, or Murder Hill.

OKAHANDJA

Situated only 70km (43 miles) north of Windhoek, this quiet town at the junction of the routes to Swakopmund at the coast and the Waterberg and Etosha in the north is usually bypassed. The town grew around a mission station which was established at a spring here in 1850.

The Herero people have deep roots in **Okahandja** and each year on a Sunday towards the end of August the town is a blaze of colour with a procession of the **Red Flag Herero**. This is an occasion not to be missed if you are in the area at the time. Women in their brilliant red traditional Victorian-style dresses and headgear and men in military-style uniforms honour their forefathers Tjamuaha, Maherero and Samuel Maherero at a communal grave and then continue to the graves of Hosea Kutako and Clemens Kapuuo, which are next to each other. To confirm the date for the procession, contact the Okahandja Municipality.

Another colourful event on the Herero calendar is the procession of the **Green Flag Herero**, or Mbanderu, who pay homage to their forefather, Kahimemua Nguvauva, on the weekend closest to the anniversary of his execution on 13 June 1896.

Kavango woodcarvers have established markets on the southern and northern sides of the town and it is worth stopping here if you are souvenir hunting.

Gross Barmen

Although often crowded over weekends, the resort, built around a **thermal spring** 24km (15 miles) west of Okahandja, is nonetheless worth a visit on your travels to the north. The spring is known for its therapeutic qualities and visitors have a choice of relaxing in the indoor thermal pool, where the water temperature is about 41°C (106°F), or the outdoor pool, which is 12°C (54°F) cooler. Those suffering from heart or kidney complaints should use the pools in moderation.

It is not only the thermal spring that is of interest here; the surroundings are worth exploring on foot. West of the dam, close to a lone palm tree, look out for the almost vanished **ruins** of a church and mission house which date back to 1871. The rocky outcrops and reedbeds surrounding the dam could prove rewarding for bird-watching, so have a pair of binoculars handy.

Accommodation at the Gross Barmen Resort ranges from the luxury of air-conditioned chalets to camp sites. Facilities include a restaurant which serves breakfast, buffet lunches and dinners, a shop and a petrol station. Contact Namibia Wildlife Resorts in Windhoek for reservations and information.

GROSS BARMEN MISSION STATION

The first mission station for the Herero people in Namibia was built around a spring in a tributary of the Okahandja River, 24km (15 miles) southwest of Okahandja. Originally known as Otjikango, meaning 'a spring flowing weakly through rocky ground', it was renamed Neu Barmen after the headquarters of the Rhenish Missionary Society in Barmen, Germany. It was later called Gross Barmen. The mission station was closed in 1890 because of fierce clashes between the Herero and the Oorlam Nama. Today, the ruins of the church and mission house are hardly visible.

Opposite: *In August each year, thousands of Herero gather in Okahandja to pay homage to their forefathers who are buried here.*
Left: *The Gross Barmen thermal spring resort, to the west of Okahandja.*

Windhoek and Surrounds at a Glance

Cool, dry winter months of **May** to **September** are best. Expect high temperatures and heavy downpours (the three gravel-surfaced roads to Namib are sometimes impassable) in summer, **November** to **March**. During **school holidays** (December/January) some restaurants and smaller shops in Windhoek are closed as locals head for the coast on holiday.

Hosea Kutako International Airport is approximately 45km (28 miles) east of city. For regular flights to and from Johannesburg, Cape Town, Luanda, Maun, Victoria Falls and Frankfurt, contact Air Namibia, tel: 061 299 6444, fax: 299 6168.

Eros Airport, just 4km (2.5 miles) from the city centre, offers regular domestic flights countrywide. A regular **transfer service** between the airport and the city centre is provided by Prime Taxi, tel: 061 272 221. Incoming flights are met by taxis. Luxury **coach services** between Walvis Bay, Swakopmund and Johannesburg, Cape Town or Victoria Falls via Windhoek are offered by Intercape Mainliner, tel: 061 227 847. Ekonolux also has a weekly service between Walvis Bay and Cape Town, tel: 064 205 935.

Windhoek is the centre of an excellent network of **tarred roads**. **Taxis** can usually be found at the rank on the corner of Fidel Castro St and Independence Avenue, or call Prime Radio Taxi, tel: 061 272 221. Many **car-hire** firms are represented in the city. In **Windhoek**, contact: Avis, tel: 061 233 166, fax: 223 072; Budget, tel: 061 228 720, fax: 227 665; Hertz, tel: 061 256 274, fax: 256 649; Imperial-Europcar, tel: 061 385 100, fax: 385 101. At **Hosea Kutako International Airport**: Avis, tel: 062 540 271, fax: 540 254; Budget, tel: 062 540 225, fax: 540 251; Hertz, tel: 062 540 115, fax: 540 117; Imperial-Europcar, tel: 062 540 040, fax: 540 389.

In Windhoek, book a **four-wheel-drive** vehicle (do it well in advance) with Avis, tel: 061 233 166, fax: 223 072; Britz, tel: 061 250 654, fax: 250 653; Camping Car Hire, tel: 061 237 756, fax: 237 757. Small **aircraft charter** and **Air Namibia** flights to Swakopmund, Walvis Bay, Lüderitz, Oranjemund, Ondangwa and Katima Mulilo leave from **Eros Airport**, 4km (2.5 miles) from city centre. Contact Air Namibia, tel: 061 299 6444, fax: 299 6168; Desert Air, tel: 061 228 101, fax: 254 345; Comav, tel: 061 227 512; Westair, tel: 061 221 091, fax: 232 778.

Windhoek
Protea Hotel Fürstenhof, Romberg Street: close to city centre, tel: 061 237 380, fax: 237 855.
Hotel Heinitzburg: elegant old castle, tel: 061 249 597.
Kalahari Sands Hotel: luxury hotel in city centre, tel: 061 280 0000, fax: 259 806.
Hotel Safari and Safari Court Hotel: 4km (2.5 miles) from city, tel: 061 296 8000, fax: 235 652.
Windhoek Country Club Resort: rural setting 7km (4 miles) from city centre, tel: 061 205 5911, fax: 252 797.
Pension Steiner: small, with private bathrooms, tel: 061 222 898, fax: 224 234.
Pension New Nouveau, quiet and personalized away from city centre in Eros, tel/fax: 061 264 319.

Mariental
Kalahari Anib Lodge, 30km (19 miles) from Mariental in Gondwana Kalahari Park; magnificent Kalahari scenery, game, drives, walks, tel: 061 230 066.

Rehoboth
Lake Oanob Resort: chalets on Oanob Dam, watersports, tel: 062 522 370, fax: 524 112.

GUEST FARMS
Heja Game Lodge, midway between the city and airport; air-conditioned rooms, restaurant overlooking dam,

Windhoek and Surrounds at a Glance

game-viewing drives, tel: 061 257 151.

Namibgrens Guest Farm, near Spreetshoogte Pass: magnificent views of the Namib, good hiking trails, tel: 062 572 021.

Windhoek

There are dozens of restaurants and coffee shops in Windhoek. Some good ones to try are:

Café Schneider, Jack Levinson Arcade: popular for light lunches, tel: 061 226 304.

Café Zoo, in Zoo Park: enjoy terrace dining with an innovative menu, tel: 061 223 479.

Hotel Fürstenhof, Romburg Street: excellent cuisine and service, tel: 061 237 380.

Joe's Beer House, 160 Nelson Mandela Avenue: open-air eatery, lots of atmosphere, tel: 061 232 457.

Gathemann, Independence Avenue: Excellent Namibian and continental cuisine, tel: 061 223 853.

Sardinia, Independence Avenue: excellent pizzas and pastas, tel: 061 225 600.

PARKS AND RESORTS

There are restaurants at Daan Viljoen, Reho Spa, Hardap and Gross Barmen.

For **safaris** from Windhoek (to destinations in Namibia and other regions in southern Africa), call Namib Travel Shop, tel: 061 274 500, 225 178, fax: 239 455.

Windhoek City tours and other day tours, including the **Gamsberg Trail**, conducted by Pack Safari, tel/fax:061 275 800. **Guided horse trails** offered by ReitSafari, tel: 061 250 764. Tours to **Sossusvlei**, **Etosha** and **Fish River Canyon** led by African Extravaganza, tel: 061 372 100.

Hire **camping equipment** from Camping Hire Namibia, Windhoek, tel: 061 252 995.

Topographical maps obtainable from Surveyor General, cnr Robert Mugabe Avenue and Dr AB May Street.

Automobile Association, corner of Independence Avenue and Fidel Castro Street, tel: 061 224 201, fax: 222 446.

Namibia Tourism, Channel Life Towers, 39 Post Street Mall, tel: 061 290 6000, fax: 254 848.

Namibia Wildlife Resorts reservation office, 189 Independence Avenue, tel: 061 285 7200, fax: 224 900.

Windhoek Tourism Information Office, Post Street Mall, tel: 061 290 2092, fax: 290 2203.

National Theatre of Namibia, tel: 061 234 633 or 374 400.

Okahandja Municipality, tel: 062 501 051.

Rehoboth Museum, tel: 062 522 954.

Shops and galleries (Windhoek): Adrian & Meyer, tel: 061 236 100; Kendzia Framing, tel: 061 225 991; Bushman Art, tel: 061 228 828; Canto Jewellers, tel: 061 222 894; Herrle & Herma, tel: 061 224 578; Holtz – Safariland, tel: 061 235 941; The House of Gems, tel: 061 225 202; Nakara, tel: 061 224 209; Namibia Crafts Centre, tel: 061 242 222; Omba Gallery, tel: 061 242 222; Leathers Unlimited, tel: 061 227 453; Rogl Souvenirs, tel: 061 225 481; Seelenbinder, tel: 061 224 230.

College of the Arts, tel: 061 374 100.

State Museum: Alte Feste, tel: 061 276 800; **Owela**, tel: 061 276 825.

Warehouse Theatre, tel: 061 225 059.

Windhoek Information and Publicity, Post Street Mall, tel: 061 290 2092, fax: 290 2203.

WINDHOEK	J	F	M	A	M	J	J	A	S	O	N	D
AVERAGE TEMP. °F	74	73	70	66	61	55	55	61	66	72	72	75
AVERAGE TEMP. °C	24	23	21	19	16	13	13	16	19	22	22	24
RAINFALL in	3	3	3	1.5	0	0	0	0	0	0.5	1	2
RAINFALL mm	78	77	79	38	7	1	1	1	3	11	27	42
DAYS OF RAINFALL	11	11	11	5	2	1	1	0	1	3	5	7

3
Southern Namibia

Southern Namibia is a vast, arid region with land-scapes ranging from the desolate Namib in the west to the rolling Kalahari dunes in the east. The gravel plains merging with the horizon, rugged mountains and fascinating geological features will enchant you. Although stark and forbidding, the terrain is especially attractive during the early morning and late afternoon when pastel shades soften the landscape.

Keetmanshoop and **Lüderitz** are the only major towns in this sparsely populated region where distances between small settlements are great. The south is well suited to small-stock farming, and most of Namibia's sheep are found here – the black-headed Dorper are reared for mutton; karakul are bred for their pelts.

Most visitors explore central and northern Namibia, so tourism in the south is fairly low-key. Recently, how-ever, several guest farms have sprung up in the region which offer visitors an opportunity to discover lesser known scenic attractions and the local way of life.

Attractions of the area range from spectacular geo-logical features such as **Brukkaros**, an extinct volcano, to the awe-inspiring **Fish River Canyon**, one of the largest in the world, to the unique **quiver tree forests** near Keetmanshoop. Along the desolate west coast lies **Lüderitz** with its romantic history of diamonds, its ghost villages and beautiful German colonial architecture.

For the adventurous, there is the tough **Fish River Canyon Backpacking Trail**, or the challenge of canoe-ing on the **Orange River**.

CLIMATE

Summers are **very hot** in the southern hinterland, with highs of over 45°C (113°F). **Winter** evenings and early mornings can be as **cold** as 4–6°C (39–41°F). **Rain** falls in summer (except in the winter-rainfall area of the southwest), with an annual mean of less than 50mm (2in) in the extreme south and 100–200mm (4–8in) further north. The **cooler coast** has average highs of 21°C (70°F) in January and 17°C (62.5°F) in July. **Wind** is not uncommon; **mist** occurs 120 days a year.

Opposite: *The rugged grandeur of the spectacu-lar Fish River Canyon.*

DON'T MISS

*** **Fish River Canyon:** among the largest in the world.
*** **Kolmanskop:** a fascinating ghost town near Lüderitz.
*** **Orange River:** a canoe trip through spectacular wilderness scenery.
** **Quiver Tree Forests:** unusually large concentrations of these tree aloes.
** **|Ai-|Ais Hot Springs:** a thermal spring situated in a strange lunar landscape.
* **Lüderitz:** a coastal town on the Diamond Coast with a distinctive German colonial atmosphere.

THE SOUTHERN HINTERLAND

South of Mariental, the road passes through what was formerly known as **Namaland**, an ethnic 'homeland' set aside by the South African government in the early 1960s for the Nama, a subgroup of the Khoikhoi people who speak the characteristic 'click' language.

Dominating the scenery to the east is a low plateau, the **Weissrand**, which stretches for over 100km (62 miles) southward. It derives its name from the white sandstone cliffs that cap the underlying shale and mudstone.

Mukurob

At the small settlement of Asab a signpost used to indicate the turnoff to **Mukurob** – one of Namibia's most popular tourist attractions until the 34m (111.5ft) high pinnacle toppled over during the night of 7 December or the early hours of 8 December 1988. The demise of this distinctive geological feature has been attributed to the gradual weakening of the narrow mudstone neck which supported a sandstone head about 12m (39ft) high – close to over a third of the height of the entire structure. It has also been suggested that the Armenian earthquake which registered strongly on the seismograph in Windhoek on the night of 7 December 1988 could have hastened its collapse.

All that remains of this well-known landmark which guarded the surrounding countryside for thousands of years are the base, a small remnant of the neck and the scattered remains of the sandstone head which was estimated to weigh about 637 tonnes.

Other names that were given to Mukurob were the Finger of God and the Afrikaans names *Vingerklip* (Finger Rock) and *Hererovrou* (Herero Woman), the latter because of its resemblance to a Herero woman's face.

Brukkaros

Further south, **Brukkaros** dominates the landscape, and even from a distance the distinctly circular, rimmed shape suggests that it is an extinct volcano. Towering some 650m (2142ft) above the plains, the crater has a diameter of

Southern Namibia

Left: *Drought-resistant quiver trees, or koker-bome, stand sentinel in the rocky wastes of the south-ern hardveld tableland.*

about 3km (2 miles) and its floor lies about 350m (1148ft) below the rim. It was formed some 80 million years ago when large areas of Namibia were gripped by a final spasm of volcanic activity.

A well-defined path that starts where the road ends at the foot of Brukkaros leads into the crater, and the view from the edge is stupendous. Intrepid walkers should set aside a full day for this fairly strenuous ramble. Alternatively, hikers can camp at the base of the crater where basic facilities are available.

Quiver Tree Forests and Giant's Playground ★★

The **quiver tree forests** at Garas and the farm Gariganus, a few kilometres from Keetmanshoop, are worth a detour. These aloes usually grow singly, or in small clumps, but here they can be found among the black dolerite out-crops, forming unusually dense concentrations. Some of the large specimens are up to 5m (16ft) high and their age is estimated at between 200 and 300 years.

Close to Gariganus is the **Giant's Playground**, where visitors can have a close-up look at the amazing forces that shaped southern Namibia millions of years ago. Numerous large boulders are stacked on top of one another, and as you make your way through them you almost expect to be confronted by a giant. These large

---

THE QUIVER TREE

In Namibia the quiver tree, or *kokerboom*, is restricted to the arid western part of the coun-try, occurring from the Orange River northward to the Brandberg. It is one of south-ern Africa's five tree aloes, and under ideal conditions it grows up to 8m (26.2ft) high. The fibrous trunk can measure up to 1m (3ft) in diameter at the base. During June and July dense masses of bright yellow flowers add a splash of colour to the landscape and provide nectar that attracts insects, birds and baboons. Sociable weavers often use these aloes as nesting sites. The distinctive quiver tree appears on the emblem of Keetmanshoop and is also depicted on the reverse side of the Namibian 50-cent coin. Its common name is derived from the San's use of the hollow branches as quivers for their arrows.

Above: *Keetmanshoop's rustic museum complex. In the foreground is a traditional Nama matjieshuis (thatched reed house).*
Opposite: *A touring party makes its way across southern Namibia's barren landscape.*

stones are remnants of dolerite which intruded into the Karoo sediment some 180 million years ago. Subsequent erosion has removed the Karoo rocks, while weathering has removed the weaker of the dolerite rocks. The stacked boulders look a bit like warts on the landscape, hence it has been given the Afrikaans name *Vratteveld*.

Keetmanshoop

Keetmanshoop, the administrative centre of Namibia's largest region, Karas, is about 500km (311 miles) south of Windhoek. The Karas region covers 161,000 km² (62,162 sq miles), or nearly one-fifth of Namibia's total surface, and is named after the Karas Mountains southeast of town. Like many settlements in Namibia, Keetmanshoop developed around the site of a mission station. The historic **Lutheran Church** in Sam Nujoma Drive was inaugurated in 1895. It has been declared a national monument, and the attractive building now serves as a museum. Various displays depict the early history of the area. Especially interesting is the traditional Nama *matjieshuis* (a house made of thatched reed) in the church grounds. The museum is open Mondays to Fridays, 07:30–12:30 and 13:30–16:30 (16:00 Fridays).

Other historic buildings in the town include the old hospital in Second Avenue, which was completed in 1913 and is also known as the **Johanitter Haus**. The

Old Post Office in the town centre, between Hampie Plichta Avenue and Sam Nujoma Drive, was completed in 1910 and the prominent steep gable and the broad rectangular tower are conspicuous features. The **Southern Tourist Forum** has its offices here and will assist visitors with the latest information on the area. Opening times are Mondays to Fridays 07:30 to 12:30 and 13:30 to 16:30 (16:00 on Fridays). Another historic building is **Schützenhaus** (1907), a former German Club and now a guesthouse.

Gondwana Cañon Park

East of the Fish River Canyon, the **Gondwana Cañon Park** covers 112,000ha (276,752 acres) of plains characterized by clumps of milkbush, granite outcrops and low mountains. Its main attractions are the spectacular scenery and open spaces. Black rhino, gemsbok, springbok, red hartebeest, Hartmann's mountain zebra, Burchell's zebra and ostrich are among the game to be seen. Activities include self-guided and guided walks, guided drives, horse-riding and mule trails in the Fish River Canyon. Accommodation ranges from chalets at Cañon Lodge and cottages at Cañon Village to rooms at Cañon Roadhouse and self-catering rooms at Cañon Mountain Camp.

BETHANIE AND AUS

Add interest to the long journey between Keetmanshoop and Lüderitz by taking a detour to **Bethanie** where a mission station to serve the Nama was established by the London Missionary Society in 1814. National monuments in the small town include **Schmelen House**, the stone walls of which date back to 1814 and that now houses a museum, the adjacent **Rhenish Mission Church** complex, and **Joseph Fredericks House**, which was erected in 1883 by the Nama chief as a council chamber and dwelling.

Just outside **Aus**, about 210km (130 miles) west of Keetmanshoop, you can see the ruins of the **First World War camp** where over 1500 German prisoners of war were held from July 1915 to May 1919.

THE FISH RIVER CANYON AND AI-AIS ***

Namibia's most spectacular geological feature, the Fish River Canyon, is within easy reach of Keetmanshoop. Over countless millennia titanic forces in the bowels of the earth and the rushing waters of the Fish River have combined to create one of the largest canyons in the world – the upper section was formed by faulting of the earth's crust, while the lower canyon was eroded by the Fish River.

Several viewpoints along the sheer edge afford awe-inspiring vistas of the canyon, which reaches a depth of up to 549m (1800ft) and a width of up to 27km (17 miles). Its entire length is 160km (99 miles), but the most impressive section stretches from just north of the main viewpoint southward for about 65km (40 miles).

Early mornings and late afternoons are the best times to visit this attraction as then you can fully appreciate the changing kaleidoscope of colours at leisure. The small camp site of **Hobas** is just a 10-minute drive from the main viewpoint at the canyon so it is a convenient place to spend the night. A clump of trees provides much appreciated shade during the day for campers, and there is also a small swimming pool where visitors can cool off. Hobas is open throughout the year. Contact Namibia Wildlife Resorts in Windhoek for reservations and information.

A stopover at the |Ai-|Ais hot-springs resort in the lower reaches of the canyon is usually on the itinerary of visitors exploring the south. Situated on the banks of the Fish River, the resort is surrounded by scenery reminiscent of a moon landscape. Accommodation

FISH RIVER CANYON BACKPACKING TRAIL

Despite its reputation of being a tough trail, the Fish River Canyon Backpacking Trail is one of the most popular routes in southern Africa and each year several thousand hikers complete the 85km (53-mile) hike. Between the start at the northernmost viewpoint near Hobas and the end of the trail at Ai-Ais, hikers have to cope with ankle-twisting boulders, stretches of soft sand and temperatures of up to 40°C (104°F), even in midwinter. The trail is only open between 15 April and 15 September, and the route should only be tackled by the fit as all food and equipment must be carried. Contact Namibia Wildlife Resorts in Windhoek for reservations and information.

ranges from fully equipped luxury flats to camping and caravan sites. Visitors have a choice of relaxing in the modern thermal hall or cooling off in the outdoor pool. Contact Namibia Wildlife Resorts in Windhoek for reservations and information.

South of Ai-Ais the Fish River continues to meander through the primitive landscape for 80km (50 miles) before joining the Orange River.

The Orange River ★★★

The Orange River forms a natural frontier with Namibia's southern neighbour, South Africa, for about 500km (311 miles). **Noordoewer**, a small settlement on the northern banks of the river, is the gateway for visitors travelling to Namibia by road from Cape Town.

Noordoewer is also the starting point of one of the most exciting adventures in Namibia – a **canoeing or rafting trip** down the Orange River. On the last part of its journey to the Atlantic Ocean this mighty waterway has carved its way through some of the most rugged terrain in southern Africa. The best way to explore this desolate and in-accessible landscape is to follow the course of the river downstream by canoe or raft. Trips last four to six days, the pace is quite relaxed and the mood is companionable.

Opposite: *A hiker on the Fish River Canyon Trail. The cliffs to either side of the canyon slash up to 549m (1800ft) deep into the plains of southern Namibia. Some of the rocks here are 2600 million years old.*
Below: *The refreshingly green-garlanded |Ai-|Ais hot-springs resort.*

Stretches of tranquil water are interrupted by white-water rapids. No canoeing experience is required and if you are not up to a rapid, you can walk around.

|Ai-|Ais/Richtersveld Transfrontier Park

The Orange River forms the northern boundary of the Richtersveld in South Africa and the southern boundary of the adjoining |Ai-|Ais Hot Springs Game Reserve in Namibia. The similarity of the geology, landscapes, flora and fauna of the two conservation areas resulted in the signing of a treaty on the establishment of a transfrontier park on 1 August 2003 by the Namibian and South African presidents. The park is managed jointly by South African National Parks and its Namibian counterpart. To encourage the free flow of visitors, the pont crossing at Sendelingsdrift was recommissioned in October 2007.

THE DIAMOND COAST

This barren, inhospitable region stretches from the Orange River mouth to just north of Lüderitz and extends about 100km (62 miles) inland from the Atlantic Ocean. The **Sperrgebiet National Park** was proclaimed in 2008 to protect the former Sperrgebiet or Forbidden Territory.

Oranjemund, at the mouth of the Orange River, is the centre of Namibia's diamond-mining industry and is unfortunately not accessible to tourists.

Lüderitz *

Lüderitz, the focal point of Namibia's Diamond Coast, is about 350km (217 miles) west of Keetmanshoop along a tarred road. There is much to do in and around this small coastal town so plan to spend at least two nights here.

The town has a notable German atmosphere which is created by the distinctive colonial-style buildings, several of which reflect the *Jugendstil* or Art Nouveau architecture of the turn of the century.

The imposing **Goerke House** on the slopes of Diamantberg (Diamond Mountain), built in 1909–10, is one of the diamond palaces that date back to the boom period of Lüderitz. It was first occupied by the Inspector of Stores, Hans Goerke, and later became the magistrate's residence. It is now used as a guest house for VIP visitors. It is open to the public from 14:00 to 16:00 Mondays to Fridays, and 16:00 to 17:00 on Saturdays and Sundays.

Opposite: *Canoeing on the Orange River past the Richtersveld National Park, which extends along the river's south bank.*
Below left: *German colonial buildings like the well-known Goerke House are a striking feature of Lüderitz.*

LÜDERITZ WATERFRONT

The N\$30 million Lüderitz Waterfront Project forms an integral part of the harbour town's atmosphere and links the central business district to the ocean. It features a combination of public open spaces, market stalls for the craft manufacturers, shops, coffee shops, restaurants, apartments and offices. Harbour Square, with its natural rock features, granite cobbles and stone, offers stunning views over the harbour, with its fishing boats, diamond vessels, yachts and flocks of noisy sea gulls. A floating pedestrian pier extends for 60m (66yd) into the harbour from the square, and there is also a small tidal pool.

ROCK LOBSTER

Lüderitz has been the centre of Namibia's rock-lobster industry since 1921. These crustaceans (often incorrectly called crayfish) favour rocky reefs at depths ranging from less than 9m (29.5ft) to more than 20m (66ft), and the main fishing grounds stretch from near the Orange River to Oyster Cliffs, 150km (93 miles) north of Lüderitz.

The fishing season usually extends from 1 November to 30 April, and the lobsters caught must have a minimum carapace length of 650mm (25.5in). The legal restriction is an attempt to protect this valuable resource from being over-exploited. Annual catches declined from over 2500 tonnes in 1983 to 130 tonnes in 1993–4, mainly as a result of over-exploitation and adverse marine conditions, but the quota for 2009 was set at 350 tonnes.

Also dominating the skyline of Diamantberg is the **Felsenkirche**, completed in 1912, which has a commanding view over Lüderitz. It is open daily at 17:00 and at 16:30 in winter – the best time of day for a visit as the beautiful stained-glass windows are then illuminated.

There are numerous other buildings worth viewing including **Kreplin House** (1909), a two-storey building with an asymmetrical façade, the houses in the **Altstadt** area in Berg Street, and the **Old Station Building,** which was completed in 1914. The small **Lüderitz Museum** in Dias Street is also interesting – opening times are 15:30 to 17:00), from Monday to Friday.

Spend a morning or afternoon exploring the **Lüderitz Peninsula**. A network of hard-surface roads is suitable for ordinary cars, but a word of caution – if you leave the road you not only risk getting stuck in loose sand, but will also do great harm to the fragile desert environment. Many delightful bays on the peninsula are worth a visit, as is the well-known **Dias Point** where Portuguese navigator Bartolomeu Dias erected a limestone cross on 25 July 1488 after he had succeeded in rounding the Cape of Good Hope. The **lighthouse** here dates back to 1910 and the **wooden bridge** was built in 1911 to provide access to the old foghorn tower that used to stand on Dias Point.

Although the water is cold, **Agate Beach**, north of the town, is an excellent place to go for swimming and surfing, and the long sandy beach is ideal for a late-afternoon stroll.

Shark Island in the bay is connected to the mainland by a causeway. A plaque near the end of the promontory was erected in honour of Adolf Lüderitz, the merchant of Bremen after whom the town

was named. The camp site here has one of the best views of any along the southern African coast, but it is often so windy that it is nearly impossible to pitch a tent. Contact Namibia Wildlife Resorts in Windhoek for reservations and information.

You can enjoy a different perspective of the Lüderitz Peninsula from the gaff-rigged schooner *Sedina*. It sets sail every morning, weather permitting, at 08:00, and on calm days continues to just off Halifax Island, giving you close-up views of the African (jackass) penguins on the island. Remember to wear suitable footwear and that it can be bitterly cold out at sea – warm clothing and a windproof anorak are essential!

Lüderitz is renowned for its sand-roses, which are crystals of gypsum and calcium sulphate salt that are also known as desert roses. They form under the sand in damp coastal conditions at Lüderitz and elsewhere along the Namib coast. You can buy specimens in shops at the town.

The Ghosts of Kolmanskop and Elizabeth Bay ★★★

Relics of the early diamond mining days can be seen at Kolmanskop, a few kilometres east of Lüderitz, and at Elizabeth Bay further south.

Following the discovery of diamonds at Grasplatz in 1908, a mining settlement sprang up at **Kolmanskop** and at the height of its growth more than 300 Germans

---

THE WATER SUPPLY OF LÜDERITZ

Obtaining fresh water at Lüderitz has always presented a problem. Early explorers got their supplies from the Nama who carried it from the interior in seal bladders and ostrich eggshells. In 1890 a seawater condenser was erected, but it could not cope with the demands of the growing settlement, and so an additional supply was shipped from Cape Town.

After the discovery of diamonds in 1908 water was at a premium and extremely expensive. When the railway line to Keetmanshoop was completed, this precious commodity was sometimes railed to the coast. However, it was as recently as 1968 that the water-supply problem was solved with the construction of a 113km (70-mile) pipeline from a borehole at Koichab Pan in the Namib Desert.

DIAMONDS

Diamonds are the largest contributor to Namibia's mining income and account for about 8% of the GDP. The industry is centred at Oranjemund, with satellite mines at Chameis and Elizabeth Bay further north and at Auchas, about 50km (31 miles) upstream of Oranjemund. Gem diamonds of high quality are mined and production averages about 1,500,000 carats a year. The alluvial deposits at Oranjemund are nearing depletion and increasing attention is being paid to offshore mining which accounts for over 60% of Namibia's total diamond production.

and approximately 800 contract labourers from the north lived here. When even richer alluvial deposits were discovered at Oranjemund, the fate of the town was sealed and in 1938 most of the mining equipment and workers were redeployed at Oranjemund. However, it was not until as late as 1956 that the last of the inhabitants finally left the abandoned settlement.

The sand dunes soon reclaimed what was rightfully theirs, burying some of the buildings of the once bustling settlement up to their roofs with sand, and giving the ghost town its distinctive character. Evidence of the lavish lifestyle of the miners can be seen in the beautifully decorated **Kasino** with its skittle alley and the remains of the splendid houses that were built for the mine manager and other senior officials.

Guided tours of Kolmanskop lasting approximately an hour are conducted from Monday to Saturday at 09:30 and 11:00, and also on Sundays and public holidays at 10:00. Permits must be obtained prior to the tour from Lüderitzbucht Safaris and Tours in Bismarck Street before driving out to the old ghost town.

Elizabeth Bay, another deserted mining settlement, lies about 30km (19 miles) south of Kolmanskop. Mining started here in 1911, and the population of the town numbered about 200 Germans and 1200 contract workers from the north of the country. Operations finally came to a halt in 1948. Subsequently, a combination of lashing winds, salt-laden mists and chemical weathering have reduced the once busy settlement to a mere skeleton – on misty days the dark brown, weatherbeaten walls of the buildings, some eroded into a honeycomb pattern and others with large chunks of plaster stripped off by the wind, create a scene of utter desolation.

In 1989 it was decided to re-establish a mine at Elizabeth Bay, and its productive life span is expected to run until 2013.

Half-day tours of the ghost town at Elizabeth Bay are conducted by Ghost Town Tours. As diamonds are still being mined in the area, bookings (at Ghost Town Tours) must be made five working days in advance so that Police clearance can be obtained.

THE BOGENFELS ARCH

Perhaps the most remarkable feature of the bleak, often mist-wreathed southern Namib shoreline is what is known as the Bogenfels, a ruggedly sculpted arched rock that rises 55m (180ft) above the Atlantic rollers. The arch – which is the highest coastal rock arch in southern Africa – once served as the terminus of a narrow-gauge private railway line that ran down the coast, linking the numerous small diamond mines of the pre-World War I era. Relics of one of the larger workings – a deposit discovered by the renowned prospector George Klinghardt – can be seen nearby.

Opposite: *One of Kolmanskop's once-splendid residences. In its heyday the diamond mining centre boasted shops, a hospital, a furniture factory, a lemonade and soda-water plant, four skittle alleys, a public swimming pool, and a grand hall complete with a theatre and an orchestra that played at tea dances. It is now a ghost town slowly being buried by the drifting sands of the desert.*
Left: *Bogenfels, a strangely sculpted rock arch on the southern Namib coast.*

BENJAMIN MORRELL

One of the first people to realize the potential of trade with the people of the interior was Benjamin Morrell, captain of the American vessel *Antarctic*. During his explorations along the Namib coast in 1828, he anchored off Ichaboe Island and discovered the rich guano deposits. When he returned to the US Morrell tried unsuccessfully to obtain financial backing for his enterprises; by the time his book *Narrative of a Voyage to the South and West Coasts of Africa* appeared in 1844, exploitation of the guano islands was already in full swing.

Below: *Plumpudding Island once played host to 400 sailing ships and a workforce of 6000.*

Namibian Islands' Marine Protected Area

The coastline to the north and south of Lüderitz is dotted with submerged reefs, rocky shoals and a string of islands, the largest being the 90ha (222-acre) Possession Island. The discovery of guano, a natural nitrate fertilizer derived from accumulated bird droppings, on these islands caused an unprecedented rush in the 1840s, and within the first year 300,000 tonnes of guano were stripped off Ichaboe Island and shipped to Britain. Guano was collected from the islands for commercial purposes until the end of 1992 when the tenders expired.

In 1861 Ichaboe was proclaimed British territory and five years later 11 other islands were also annexed by Britain. (However, numerous smaller islets and outcrops with names such as Dumfudgeon, Black Sophie and Boat Rock were never proclaimed British territory.) Sovereignty over the annexed areas was transferred to the Cape Colony in 1874. Collectively known as the Penguin Islands, some of them were given colourful names such as Plumpudding and Roast Beef (or Sinclair's), while others were simply descriptive names (Long Island) or referred to specific mammals (Seal Island) or birds (Albatross Rock). The islands and the enclave of Walvis Bay were reintegrated into Namibia at midnight on 28 February 1994.

The islands were reintegrated into Namibia on 1 March 1994 and lie within the Namibian Islands' Marine Protected Area proclaimed in 2009. The islands are important breeding sites for African penguin and other sea birds and access is restricted. Good views of the penguin colony on Halifax Island can, however, be enjoyed from Halifax Point on the Lüderitz Peninsula if you have a good pair of binoculars.

Southern Namibia at a Glance

BEST TIMES TO VISIT

Summers are very hot in the south of the country, so **May** to **September** is the best time to visit. **February** to **May** is pleasant on the coast, but it is quite cool throughout the year; expect mist year-round and also wind in **August**.

GETTING THERE

There are several scheduled **Air Namibia** flights a week to Lüderitz, tel: 061 299 6444, fax: 299 6168. A regular **coach service** beween Windhoek and Cape Town and Johannesburg stops at Rehoboth, Mariental and Keetmanshoop. For information contact Intercape Mainliner, tel: 061 227 847. For the budget traveller, TransNamib offers a regular passenger **train** service between Windhoek and Keetmanshoop, tel: 061 298 2175, and also a twice-weekly **bus** service between Keetmanshoop and Lüderitz, tel: 061 298 2175.

GETTING AROUND

Tarred roads link Keetmanshoop with Lüderitz and Noordoewer. **Gravel-surface roads** generally in good condition and negotiable by car.

WHERE TO STAY

Aus

Klein-Aus Vista, just west of Aus: guided horse trails, hiking, guided tours to wild horses of the Namib, wide range of accommodation; tel: 063 258 021, fax: 258 021.

Fish River Canyon Area

Accommodation in the Gondwana Cañon Park near the Fish River Canyon ranges from chalets nestling amongst granite boulders at **Cañon Lodge** and cottages at **Cañon Village** to double rooms at the **Cañon Roadhouse** and self-catering rooms at **Cañon Mountain Camp**. Activities include self-guided and guided walks, guided drives, horse-riding and mule trails in the Fish River Canyon; tel: 061 230 066, fax: 251 863.

Keetmanshoop

Birds Mansions Hotel: tel: 063 221 711, fax: 221 730.
Birds Nest Guesthouse: tel: 063 222 906, fax: 222 261.

Lüderitz

Nest Hotel: tel: 063 204 000, fax: 204 001.
Protea Hotel Zum Sperrgebiet: tel: 063 203 411, fax: 203 414.

WHERE TO EAT

Lüderitz

Ritzi's: seafood and steaks, tel: 063 202 818.
Penguin Restaurant, Nest Hotel: seafood restaurant with sea view, tel: 063 204 000.

TOURS AND EXCURSIONS

For **Orange River canoe trips** contact Felix Unite, tel: +27 21 702 9400, fax: 702 9493. Half-day tours of **Elizabeth Bay ghost town** are run by Ghost Town Tours, tel: 063 204 031; day tours of **Pomona ghost town** and **Bogenfels rock arch** are run by Coastways, tel: 063 202 002; apply at least five days in advance for Police clearance. For **Sedina yacht trips** and other tours book with Lüderitzbuch Safaris & Tours.

USEFUL TELEPHONE NUMBERS

Lüderitz Museum, tel: 063 202 532. **Ministry of Environment and Tourism**, Lüderitz, tel: 063 202 811. **Lüderitzbucht Safaris and Tours**, tel: 063 202 719.

LÜDERITZ BAY	J	F	M	A	M	J	J	A	S	O	N	D
AVERAGE TEMP. °F	64	64	64	63	61	59	57	57	57	59	61	63
AVERAGE TEMP. °C	18	18	18	17	16	15	14	14	14	15	16	17
SEA TEMP. °F	68	66	64	63	63	59	59	59	59	59	61	61
SEA TEMP. °C	20	19	18	17	17	15	15	15	15	15	16	16
RAINFALL in	0	0	0	0	0	0	0	0	0	0	0	0
RAINFALL mm	1	1	2	2	2	3	2	2	1	1	1	1
DAYS OF RAINFALL	1	1	1	1	1	1	0	1	1	0	1	0
DAYS OF MIST/FOG	10	12	13	13	11	9	7	8	9	7	9	10

4
The Namib

The **Namib** is one of the most fascinating places on earth and home to a wide variety of desert-adapted plants and animals that are found nowhere else in the world. Stretching all the way from the Olifants River in South Africa to the southwestern parts of Angola, the most spectacular section of the desert lies between Lüderitz and Swakopmund.

The scenery varies from gravel plains with rocky outcrops in the south to the inhospitable sand sea of the central Namib and the flat gravel plains north of the Kuiseb River, which is choked by the encroaching dunes before it can reach the Atlantic Ocean at **Walvis Bay**.

Although entry to the Namib sand sea is prohibited because of the inhospitable terrain, many areas are still surprisingly accessible, even to ordinary cars.

Covering 4,976,800ha (12,298,170 acres), the **Namib-Naukluft Park** is the third largest game reserve in Africa and amongst the largest in the world.

Swakopmund, with its distinctive German colonial atmosphere, is a convenient base from which to explore the gravel plains and rugged Kuiseb Canyon in the **Namib** section of the park. It is also close to the **Walvis Bay Lagoon** and **Sandwich Harbour**, two of the most important wetlands along the west coast of Africa.

Contrasting sharply with the gravel plains are the rugged **Naukluft Mountains** with their crystal-clear pools, the spectacular dunes of **Sossusvlei** and **Sesriem Canyon** where the Tsauchab River has exposed millions of years of geological history.

CLIMATE

Though **coastal** temperatures are **moderate** – an average minimum of 9°C (48°F) in midwinter and maximum of 23°C (73°F) in **summer** – early mornings and late afternoons are often **misty** and cool. The mean annual rainfall is only 15mm (0.6in); precipitation is nearly always in the form of **fog**.

Further inland, daily temperatures are **moderate** in **winter** with a low of 5°C (41°F), but **highs in summer** exceed 35°C (95°F). The Naukluft Mountains get **summer rains** – about 195mm (7.6in) a year.

Opposite: *The searing sands at Sossusvlei.*

DON'T MISS

*** Balloon Safari: a bird's-eye view of the Namib Desert.
*** Sossusvlei: spectacular sand dunes of the Namib.
** Welwitschia Drive: scenic interpretative drive.
** Swakopmund: German colonial buildings.
* Naukluft Mountains: rugged scenery, day walks and hiking trails.

THE COAST

The 250km (155-mile) stretch between Walvis Bay and the Ugab River is the most accessible part of the Namib coast. Swakopmund, Henties Bay and Walvis Bay are popular holiday destinations, and excellent conditions for angling are a main attraction. Of interest is the salt-surface road which leads northward from Swakopmund.

Swakopmund **

Swakopmund with its distinctly German atmosphere (many locals speak German) is the country's most popular holiday resort, especially during the summer when thousands of Namibians flock to the coast to escape the intense heat of the interior. Just before you reach the town, along the B2 route, you will notice an old steam engine that is bound to rouse your curiosity. It came to a grinding halt here shortly after it was imported from Germany in 1896, hence the name **Martin Luther** after the Reformation leader who stated 'Here I stand, God help me, I cannot do otherwise'.

German colonial-style buildings dating back to the early 1900s still dominate the town. Notable are the **Swakopmund railway station** (1901) in Theo-Ben Gurirab Avenue, one of the finest in southern Africa, **Woermannhaus** (1905), built in *Fachwerkbau* style, in Bismarck Street, and **Hohenzollernhaus** (1906) with its high mansard roof, elaborate mouldings and statue of Atlas. The **State House** (originally called Kaiserliches Bezirksgericht) next to the **lighthouse** was finished in 1902 as a magistrate's court. It is now the residence of the President during the Cabinet recess in December/January.

Take a ramble through the town to see the beautiful buildings, and visit the **Namib-i** office, corner of Sam Nujoma Avenue and Hendrik Witbooi Street, open Monday to Friday

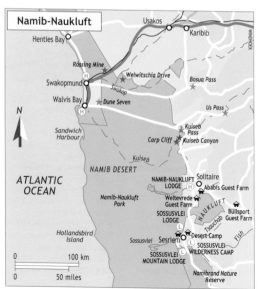

Left: *Hohenzollernhaus, one of the many graceful colonial buildings of Swakopmund, a seaside resort surrounded on three sides by the vast Namib Desert. The nearby saltpans are famed for their variety of coastal and aquatic birds.*

08:00 to 13:00 and 14:00 to 17:00, Saturday 09:00 to 13:00 and 15:00 to 17:00, Sunday 09:00 to 13:00. Ask for the key to the **Damara Tower** of **Woermannhaus** at Swakop Info (in the base of the tower) for a view of the town. The **Swakopmund Art Association Gallery** in Woermannhaus is open Mondays to Fridays 10:00 to 12:00 and 15:00 to 16:00 and Saturdays 10:00 to 12:00. Swakopmund's landmark **jetty** is a good place to see the sunset. Built in 1911–15, it was planned to be 640m (2100ft) long, but only reached 262m (859,5ft). The first section has been renovated and the seaward section has also been saved from demolition – with a planned restaurant at its end.

Don't miss the mouthwatering German confectionery at **Café Anton** and **Café Treff**, or the variety of German breads – like Berliner (rye bread) and brötchens (bread rolls) – and cakes baked daily at **Putensen Backerei**.

The **Swakopmund Museum** in Strand Street is one of the most interesting in Namibia. Exhibits include a display of the early history of Swakopmund, archaeological and ethnological displays, a reconstruction of the old Adler Pharmacy and a fascinating collection of minerals. Daily opening times are 10:00 to 17:00.

Not to be missed are the **National Marine Aquarium** in Strand Street and the **Kristall Galerie**, corner of Tobias Hainyeko Street and Theo-Ben Gurirab Avenue, which houses the largest known crystal cluster in the world.

Although **Palm Beach** is safe for swimming, the water is usually too cold for anything more than a quick dip.

BEST BUYS IN SWAKOPMUND

- Karakul rugs and wall hangings from Karakulia.
- Handcrafted leather goods from African Leather Creations (previously Swakopmund Tannery).
- Paintings by local artists from Die Muschel and the Hobby Horse.
- A variety of gemstones from Stonetique.
- Handcrafted jewellery from African Art Jewellers and Engelhard Design.
- Namibian ethnic artefacts and colonial-period antiques from Peter's Antiques.
- Local first-day covers and stamps from Namib Stamps.

BIRD ISLAND

The large wooden platform built on Bird Island, about 7km (4 miles) north of Walvis Bay, is a familiar landmark along the coastal road. Built in 1930 by a Swakopmund carpenter, K. H. A. Winter, to collect guano from the thousands of birds that used to roost on the rocks at low tide, the platform originally measured 16m² (172 sq ft). It has been extended several times; the structure is now 17,000m² (182,988 sq ft) and is supported by no less than 1000 freestanding stilts. It provides a roosting and nesting place for thousands of Cape cormorants and smaller numbers of pelicans and other seabirds. Guano is collected during February and March, and is brought ashore by a motor-driven cableway. Annual production varies from 200 to 1000 tonnes.

Outings from Swakopmund

Earlier this century camels were widely used by the Police in Namibia as a means of transport; today they no longer serve this practical purpose. The **Camel Farm** about 12km (7.5 miles) east of Swakopmund, run by Mrs Elke Erb, offers the novelty of camel rides in the afternoon. It is best to make a reservation.

An interesting excursion from Swakopmund is a visit to the world's largest opencast uranium mine, **Rössing**, some 55km (34 miles) east of Swakopmund. Tours are conducted on the first and third Friday of the month. Book at the Swakopmund Museum.

The coast to the north and south of Swakopmund offers several opportunities to birders. Among the most noteworthy species to be seen here are the Damara tern, chestnut-banded plover, white pelican and a variety of summer migrants.

Long Beach and Dolphin Park

The coast south of Swakopmund is well frequented by anglers, and pelicans are often seen waiting patiently near fishermen for scraps of fish. The two modern resorts halfway between Swakopmund and Walvis Bay are very popular. The facilities at Long Beach include

Opposite: *The lagoon to the south of Walvis Bay is home to 50 different kinds of waterbird. These are among the 20,000 or so flamingoes that can be seen here at any one time.*
Right: *Camel rides are a popular attraction on a farm near Swakopmund. These exotic animals were used for desert transport in the early days.*

a fishing jetty, tidal pools, a trendy restaurant, various campfire places and camp sites. Dolphin Park, 3km (2 miles) further south, has been laid out like a park with a sports and a tidal pool, a waterslide, campfire places and a cafeteria.

Walvis Bay

Hemmed in by the Atlantic Ocean on the seaboard side and the golden-yellow dunes of the Namib further inland, **Walvis Bay** lies on a lagoon. The town is the centre of Namibia's lucrative fishing industry and also the country's only deep-sea port, so it is mainly a commercial settlement. It is also the largest producer of salt in Africa. The **Walvis Bay Salt Works** are situated to the south of the town, but they are not open to the public.

A familiar sight here is that of a flock of both greater and lesser flamingoes taking to the air from the lagoon, where they like to feed. The former species is taller, is white in colour and has a pink bill with a black tip; the latter is pink in colour and has a dark maroon bill.

Walvis Bay Wetlands ★★

The Walvis Bay wetlands, comprising the lagoon, salt works and western shores, are among the 10 most important coastal wetlands in Africa and supports up to 161,000 birds during summer and up to 68,000 in winter. Among the most common Palaearctic migrants are curlew sandpipers, sanderlings and little stints, while greater and lesser flamingoes account for more than 90% of the intra-African migrants. Low tide is generally the best time for bird-watching.

A novel way of exploring the lagoon is to join a **sea kayak tour** offered by Jeanne Meintjies of Eco-Marine Kayak Tours. Tours of varying duration are available

HISTORY OF WALVIS BAY

12 March 1878: port and surrounding country proclaimed British territory.
7 August 1884: port and settlement declared part of Cape Colony.
31 May 1910: incorporation of Walvis Bay into Union of South Africa.
30 September 1922: Walvis Bay placed under control of Administration of South West Africa.
31 August 1977: administration of Walvis Bay reverts back to Cape Province.
21 March 1990: independent Namibia's Constitution becomes effective, but South Africa still maintains sovereignty over Walvis Bay and offshore islands.
1 November 1992: joint administration of territory by Namibia and South Africa established.
1 March 1994: finally, Walvis Bay enclave and offshore islands reintegrated into Namibia.

Above: *The barren seaboard of the central Namib.*

and they offer kayakers the opportunity to view the seals and other marine species at close quarters.

Dune Sports

The dunes between Swakopmund and Walvis Bay are ideally suited to a variety of dune sports, with paragliding and sand-boarding being the most popular. Although the dunes are relatively low when compared to those of Sossusvlei, sand-boarders can easily reach speeds of up to about 80kph (50mph). Guided quad-bike tours of the dunes, conducted from Swakopmund and Long Beach Resort, provide an adrenaline rush.

Dune Seven

Although not nearly as impressive as the sand dunes at Sossusvlei, **Dune Seven**, a few kilometres east of Walvis Bay along the Rooikop road, is the most easily accessible dune along this stretch of the coast. A scramble to the crest of the dune, approximately 50m (163ft) high, will not only make you aware of how tiring walking in the thick loose sand is but will also give you a bird's-eye view of the dune fields. Picnic facilities are available here for day visitors.

THE NAMIB-NAUKLUFT PARK

The Namib Desert has a surprising variety of landscape types. The section of the park between Lüderitz and the Kuiseb River is characterized by massive sand dunes, while the Namib section, between the Kuiseb and Swakop rivers, consists of vast quartzite gravel plains, bounded on the seaward side by a strip of dunes. Other components of the park include Sandwich, one of the most important coast wetlands in Africa, and the rugged Naukluft Mountains along the eastern edge of the desert.

Sandwich Harbour

In the early days of sail this lagoon, about 45km (30 miles) south of Walvis Bay, provided a safe anchorage to passing ships, hence it was called **Sandwich Harbour**. It has long since stopped serving this purpose, and is now a haven for a variety of birds.

Over the past 25 years the lagoon has been subject to dramatic natural changes. The reed-lined freshwater pools at its northern end have long since disappeared, while dynamic coastal processes have altered the nature of the coastline. What used to be a relatively easy drive to Sandwich should now be attempted only by experienced 4x4 drivers and only after obtaining local advice.

About 97% of the up to 238,000 waders, terns, cormorants, flamingoes and pelicans attracted to the wetlands of Sandwich Harbour are found on the mudflats to the south and the sandspit to the west of the lagoon. Both areas are, however, too far south for casual visits.

Sandwich Harbour is only accessible by four-wheel-drive, and vehicles are not allowed past the southern boundary of the angling area, so those who want to explore the lagoon will have to undertake a 1.5- to 2-hour walk from there. No overnight camping is allowed. Permits to visit Sandwich Harbour can be obtained from Namibia Wildlife Resorts in Swakopmund, or Windhoek.

> ### DESERT DO'S AND DON'TS
>
> The ecology of the Namib Desert is very fragile, and any unnecessary disturbance can cause irreparable damage. **Off-road driving** is especially cause for concern – tracks are unsightly and can scar the landscape for 50 years or more; the unique lichen fields of the Namib are destroyed; and the rare Damara tern, which breeds in the National West Coast Recreation Area, is threatened (*see* page 79). Always follow existing tracks.
>
> Visitors must not collect any archaealogical artefacts, plants or plant material. Always carry a supply of wood with you when **camping** in the desert. Only use established camp sites, and always remove all your litter.

Below left: *Coastal birds in flight over the unspoilt Sandwich Harbour.*
Below: *A curlew sandpiper.*

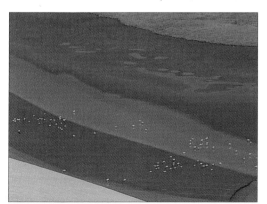

WELWITSCHIA

This botanical curiosity is restricted to the Namib Desert, from the Kuiseb River in the south to southwestern Angola. Although it has characteristics of both flowering and cone-bearing plants, it is classified as a Gymnosperm, an ancient plant order which includes cycads and conifers.

The tangled leaf-mass creates the impression that the plant has numerous leaves, but only two are produced. There are separate male and female plants; the female variety bear greenish-yellow cones banded with reddish brown that are larger than the salmon-coloured cones of the male. Average-sized specimens are between 500 and 600 years old, while the **Giant Welwitschia** is estimated to be about 2000 years old.

Namib Section ★★

Between the Kuiseb and Swakop rivers stretch sparsely vegetated gravel plains, occasionally interrupted by *inselbergen* (isolated remnant mountains).

In the shimmering midday heat mirages create visions of a massive lake on the horizon, a lone gemsbok takes on a grotesque shape and the plains seem totally devoid of life. Yet, the Namib is home to several fascinating animals and plants, all adapted to survive in the desert. Among the game to be seen here are herds of springbok, gemsbok, Hartmann's mountain zebra and bat-eared fox, as well as ostrich.

This section of the Namib-Naukluft Park is traversed by a network of well-maintained gravel roads which are negotiable by car (unless a signpost indicates otherwise). There are a number of picnic places for day visitors, as well as several delightful camp sites. However, facilities are limited to fireplaces and pit latrines.

Visitors may travel through the park on the proclaimed roads, but must obtain a permit to explore the signposted tourist roads (including the Welwitschia Drive) or to camp. Contact Namibia Wildlife Resorts in Windhoek or Swakopmund, weekdays.

One of the best ways to learn more about this fascinating area is to follow the 140km (87-mile) **Welwitschia Drive**. This self-guided interpretative route starts about 20km (12 miles) from Swakopmund and features the geology, lichens and some of

the interesting plants, including notable specimens of the *Welwitschia mirabilis*, of the Namib. The appropriately named **Moon Landscape** flanking the Swakop River Valley was formed over millions of years when the river's thousands of tributaries incised deeply into the soft deposits laid down about 450 million years ago.

Left: *The barren landscape of the Kuiseb Canyon.*
Opposite: *The strange welwitschia plant lives for more than 1000 years and produces just two leaves, which grow continuously, constantly splitting into ribbon-like strips.*

Kuiseb Canyon

Rising in the Khomas Hochland near Windhoek, the **Kuiseb River** has carved a spectacular canyon where it enters the Namib-Naukluft Park, about 165km (103 miles) from Swakopmund and about 230km (143 miles) from Windhoek. It is a wild landscape of badlands, crisscrossed by a maze of dry river courses which eventually make their way to the Kuiseb River.

The river is often dry for several years, but after heavy rains in the highlands it is transformed into a seething mass of water which rushes through a barren landscape. Floods wash away the sand that has been blown into the riverbed and thus the Kuiseb River plays an important role in preventing the sand dunes from encroaching onto the flat gravel plains that spread northward to the Swakop River. Subsequently, the river can flow for anything from a few days to over 100 days. The pools in the middle reaches supply water for gemsbok, Hartmann's mountain zebra, klipspringer and even the three troops of baboons which eke out an existence here.

About 9km (5.5 miles) west of the Kuiseb River camp site a signpost indicates the turnoff to **Carp Cliff**, overlooking the canyon far below. The view from here is spectacular in the late afternoon when the canyon walls take on a fiery orange hue in the last rays of the sun.

THE SHELTERING DESERT

A short walk from the viewpoint at **Carp Cliff** leads to a large overhang which has been immortalized in the classic book, *The Sheltering Desert*. During World War II two German geologists, Henno Martin and Herman Korn, who feared being interned, decided to flee into the desert rather than become involved in the war. Carp Cliff was the first of their three hideouts during the two-and-a-half years they spent in the Namib.

Their attempts at supplementing their meagre rations by hunting, collecting honey, fishing and growing vegetables in the Kuiseb river bed are related in the book, written by Henno Martin.

BALLOON FLIGHTS

An unusual and unforgettable way of seeing the gravel plains, *inselbergen* and dunes of the Namib is to undertake a **balloon flight** from the Sesriem area, or from the NamibRand Nature Reserve south of Sesriem. Takeoff is just after sunrise and after drifting in the air for about an hour a champagne breakfast is served in the middle of the desert. Accommodation is available at several lodges in this area.

Below: *Ballooning over the southern Namib, not far from Sesriem in the Namib-Naukluft Park.*

Naukluft Mountains *

Situated on the edge of the Namib, about 347km (216 miles) from Swakopmund and about 240km (149 miles) from Windhoek, the **Naukluft Mountains** form part of the dramatic escarpment which separates the coastal plain from the inland plateau. It is an extremely rugged mountain range, characterized by sheer cliffs, deeply incised river valleys and rolling hills.

The Naukluft complex was originally proclaimed as a sanctuary for the Hartmann's mountain zebra. Other large mammals found here include gemsbok, springbok, kudu, klipspringer and steenbok; the park also supports a healthy leopard population. To enable the gemsbok to migrate freely between the mountains and the dune sea further west, the complex is connected to the rest of the Namib-Naukluft Park by means of a narrow corridor.

Facilities here are limited to a few camp sites with ablutions; advance reservations with Namibia Wildlife Resorts in Windhoek are essential. The rugged terrain is inaccessible to sedan cars, but there is a challenging two-day **4x4 trail** over 72km (45 miles). A secluded overnight camp provides accommodation at the end of the first day's drive. There are two **one-day hikes** for the more energetic, while the **Naukluft Hiking Trail** caters for the adventurous. The latter is a tough route with several options ranging from a four-day hike to a 120km (74.5-mile) eight-day circular route. The trail traverses difficult terrain and should not be attempted by inexperienced or unfit hikers or those who do not have a head for heights. On three sections of the trail, chains assist hikers up or down waterfalls. Two of the overnight huts along the trail are converted farmhouses that are equipped with bunks and mattresses, while basic stone shelters without any facilities (except water) are provided at the six other overnight stops. Because of the heat in this part of the world, hiking is permitted only from 1 March to the third Friday in October and groups may consist of only 3–12 people. Contact Namibia Wildlife Resorts in Windhoek for reservations. This is a tough trail.

Above: *Desert reptiles include the Fitzsimmons' burrowing skink.*

The Namib Dune Sea

South of the Kuiseb River is the Namib's vast **sea of dunes** ranging from the transverse dunes along the coast to the star dunes near the eastern edge of the desert.

Among the fascinating **animals** which are endemic to the Namib are the side-winding adder, the almost translucent web-footed gecko, the Namib golden mole and a host of *toktokkie*, or tenebrionid, beetles. To survive in this inhospitable environment where temperatures soar over 40°C (104°F), these desert creatures have adapted in several ways. They live underground where temperature fluctuations are minimal, or climb onto plants to escape from the hot surface of the sand. Fundamental to their survival are the dense banks of fog which supplement the meagre rainfall, and the desert-adapted beetles collect the precipitation from the fog in a variety of ways. Some beetle species dig shallow trenches to trap the fog, while others obtain their water by doing a headstand, facing the fog-laden wind, so that water droplets trickle down into their mouths.

Another key to the survival of the smaller desert animals is detritus, which consists of windblown plant material, dead insects and animal droppings. Detritus forms the basis of the food of the detritivores, like the tenebrionid beetle, which in turn provide a source of food for a host of carnivores, like Anchieta's dune lizard, which in turn is preyed on by the side-winding adder.

MOUNTAIN ZEBRA

The **Hartmann's mountain zebra** is closely related to the Cape mountain zebra, which occurs much further south in the Eastern Cape Midlands and the mountains separating the Little and Great Karoo. The range of the Hartmann's mountain zebra extends from the Orange River northward along the escarpment into southwestern Angola and eastwards into the Khomas Hochland in central Namibia and the western part of the Etosha National Park. One of the major differences between the two mountain zebras is that the dark and light stripes of Hartmann's are more or less equally wide, while the dark stripes of the Cape mountain zebra are much wider than the lighter stripes. The former is also slightly taller than the southern subspecies.

Above: *The Sesriem camp site at sunrise.*

Sesriem and Sossusvlei ★★★

A visit to Sesriem, the gateway to Sossusvlei, one of Namibia's prime tourist attractions, is well worth the drive of 350km (218 miles) from Swakopmund, or 330km (205 miles) from Windhoek. Facilities at **Sesriem** at the edge of the dunes, are limited to camp sites shaded by camel thorn trees, ablutions, a shop, filling station and swimming pool. Contact Namibia Wildlife Resorts in Windhoek for reservations.

The **Sossusvlei Lodge** adjacent to Sesriem offers accommodation in canvas- and adobe-walled double-bed units. In addition the lodge has a restaurant, alfresco dining terrace, bar and swimming pool.

Some 4km (2.5 miles) south of Sesriem the **Tsauchab River** has carved a deep, narrow canyon through the con-glomerates and after good rains the pools in the canyon retain their water for several months. Sesriem means 'six thongs' in Afrikaans and the name refers to the way the early pioneers in the region drew water from the pools by lowering a bucket tied to the end of six ox-thongs.

From Sesriem a tar road follows the Tsauchab valley past the much-photographed Dune 45 to reach the 2x4 parking area after 60km (37 miles). The last 5km (3 miles) of the road to **Sossusvlei** is through heavy sand, suitable only for a four-wheel-drive. The vlei, a greyish-white clay pan which is virtually surrounded by towering orange sand dunes, is often dry for several years, but after good rains the Tsauchab River sometimes floods the vlei.

Though the dunes are impressive – they measure up to 325m (1066ft) – it should be borne in mind that they are not freestanding as they rest on a sandstone terrace.

An early start is advisable as the colour transformation of the dunes is at its best immediately after sunrise. Also, early mornings are the best time to attempt to scale one of the dunes in the vicinity of Sossusvlei (a daunting undertaking!). A few picnic sites under tall camel thorn trees are available at the vlei, as well as toilets.

Up-market accommodation near the park is available at **Sossusvlei Wilderness Camp**. The stone, timber and thatch chalets are built among the boulders of a rocky outcrop with breathtaking views over the surrounding plains.

NamibRand Nature Reserve

Covering some 200,000ha (494,200 acres) of plains, magnificent dunes, granite outcrops and mountains, this reserve lies 26km (16 miles) south of Sesriem as the crow flies. To the west, it borders on the Namib-Naukluft Park for over 120km (75 miles), while the Nubib Mountains lie to the east. Home to herds of gemsbok, springbok, zebra and a host of smaller creatures, the reserve's main attractions are its awe-inspiring scenery and solitude. Activities include scenic drives and guided walks. Balloon safaris are operated in the reserve and accommodation is available in three luxury camps and a rustic farmhouse.

> ### ENDEMIC ANIMALS OF THE NAMIB
>
> The Namib is home to several creatures which are not found anywhere else in the world. More than 20 kinds of **tok-tokkie**, or **tenebrionid**, **beetles** have adapted to the virtually barren dunes, while some species only occur on the gravel plains north of the Kuiseb River. Among the endemic animals are **Grant's golden mole** and two gerbil species – **Setzer's hairy-footed gerbil** and the **dune hairy-footed gerbil**. The dunes of the northern Namib are the habitat of **Skoog's lizard**, a vegetarian lizard which escapes to safety by diving into the sand in a corkscrew motion. Two endemic bird species are the **dune lark**, found in the sand dunes, and **Gray's lark** of the gravel plains.

Below: *Neatly corrugated landscape at Sossusvlei.*

The Namib at a Glance

BEST TIMES TO VISIT

The temperate months of **October** to **March** best time to visit **coast**, but occasional hot, dry easterly winds. Cooler months from **May** to **September** best time to visit **Namib**, but strong easterly winds bring high temperatures.

GETTING THERE

Air Namibia operates several scheduled weekly flights between Walvis Bay and Windhoek, tel: 061 299 6444. Small **air charters** operate from Swakopmund and Walvis Bay. TransNamib operates six overnight passenger **train** services between Windhoek and Walvis Bay a week, tel: 061 298 2175. Intercape Mainliner offers **coach service** between Windhoek and Walvis Bay several times a week, tel: 061 227 847.
Swakopmund is 350km (217 miles) from Windhoek along a **tarred road**. **Gravel-surface roads** between Lüderitz or Maltahöhe and Walvis Bay or Swakopmund are generally in quite a good condition.

GETTING AROUND

Most of the popular tourist attractions in the Namib are accessible by car along **gravel-surface roads**, generally in good condition. However, unless you are with an organized tour or safari, make sure you have basic spares, water and a second spare wheel as some of the back roads in this remote area carry very little traffic.
Car hire in Swakopmund – Avis, tel: 064 402 527; Budget, tel: 064 463 380; Imperial-Europcar, tel: 064 400 383; Hertz, tel: 064 461 826. In Walvis Bay – Avis, tel: 064 402 527; Budget, tel: 064 204 128; Imperial-Europcar, tel: 064 207 391, fax: 207 407.

WHERE TO STAY

Swakopmund
Hansa Hotel: tel: 064 414 200, fax 414 299.
Hotel Europa Hof: tel: 064 405 061, fax: 402 391.
Beach Lodge: tel: 064 400 933, fax: 400 934.
Brigadoon B&B: tel: 064 406 064, fax: 464 195.
Swakopmund Hotel and Entertainment Centre: tel: 064 410 5200, fax: 410 5360.

Namib-Naukluft Park Area
Büllsport Guest Farm, at foot of Naukluft Mountains: walking trails, horse riding, four-wheel-drive trips to nearby attractions, tel: 063 693 371.
Desert Camp, self-catering camp with central communal area, 4km from Sesriem; tel: 061 693 205, fax: 693 231.
Sossusvlei Lodge, adjacent to Sesriem, tel: +27 21 930 4564, fax: +27 21 930 4574.
Namib-Naukluft Lodge, bordering Namib-Naukluft Park: trips to Sossusvlei, tel: 061 372 100.
Hauchabfontein Camping, on Tsauchab River in the Naukluft: delightful camp sites, tel/fax: 063 293 433.
Sossusvlei Wilderness Camp, close to Sossusvlei: luxury accommodation, ballooning, trips to Sossusvlei, tel: 061 274 500, fax: 239 455.
Weltevrede Guest Farm, at the foot of the Naukluft Mountains: close to Sossusvlei, typical Namibian hospitality, tel: 063 683 073, fax: 683 074.
NamibRand Nature Reserve, adjoining Namib-Naukluft Park: three accommodation options, tel: 061 230 616, fax: 220 102.

Walvis Bay
Lagoon Lodge, 88 Kovambo Nujoma Drive: tel: 064 200 850, fax: 200 851.
Langholm Hotel Garni, 24 2nd Street West: tel: 064 209 230, fax: 209 430.
Protea Hotel Walvis Bay, cnr Sam Nujoma Avenue and 10th Rd: tel: 064 209 560, fax: 209 565.

WHERE TO EAT

Swakopmund
Café Anton, Bismarck Street: for tea, coffee and light meals, tel: 064 400 331.
Erich's, Daniël Tjongarero Street: for seafood (fresh linefish, rock lobster and oysters), tel: 064 405 141.
Kucki's Pub, Tobias Haiyenko Street: a popular pub with an informal, busy atmosphere and some really excellent

The Namib at a Glance

food, tel: 064 402 407.

Platform One Restaurant, Swakopmund Hotel and Entertainment Centre: excellent buffet and à la carte restaurant, tel: 064 410 5200.

Putensen Bakery and Café, Sam Nujoma Avenue: for tea, coffee and light snacks, tel: 064 402 034.

The Tug, The Jetty: a bar in an authentic tug: excellent seafood and ocean views, tel: 064 402 356.

Western Saloon, Tobias Haiyenko Street: small, but offers personalized service; renowned for seafood and steaks, tel: 064 405 395.

Walvis Bay
The Raft Restaurant, Esplanade: good food and excellent views over Walvis Bay lagoon, tel: 064 204 877.

TOURS AND EXCURSIONS

For half- and full-day tours of **Swakopmund**, **Walvis Bay, Namib Desert**, **Sandwich Lagoon** and **Cape Cross** contact Charly's Desert Tours, tel: 064 404 341; Swakop Tour Company, tel: 064 404 088. Scenic **Balloon flights** are operated from NamibRand and the Sesriem area by Namib Sky Adventure Safaris, tel: 063 683 188, fax: 683 189.

For **angling trips**, from rock-surf to deep-sea fishing, contact Sunrise Tours, tel: 064 404 561 (in Swakopmund).

For **dolphin and seal cruises**, contact Mola Mola Safaris in Walvis Bay, tel: 064 205 511.

Flights over areas along the coast that are inaccessible by vehicle, as well as over the Namib Desert, including Sossusvlei and further afield, offered by Pleasure Flights, Sam Nujoma Avenue, Swakopmund, tel and fax: 064 404 500, and in Walvis Bay by Bay Air, 242 11th Street, tel: 064 204 319.

For **sea kayak trips** on Walvis Bay Lagoon contact Jeanne Meintjies in Walvis Bay, tel and fax: 064 203 144.

Camel Farm, tel: 064 400 363.

USEFUL TELEPHONE NUMBERS

Namibia Wildlife Resorts, Woermann House, Am Ankerplatz, Swakopmund, tel: 064 402 172.

Namibia Wildlife Resorts, Windhoek, tel: 061 285 7200 for reservations and information, fax: 224 900.

Namib-i information office, Sam Nujoma Avenue, Swakopmund, tel: 064 404 827.

Shops and galleries (Swakopmund): African Art Jewellers, Hansa Hotel Building, Hendrik Witbooi Street, tel: 064 405 566; African Kirikara Art, Am Ankerplatz, tel: 064 463 146; Casa Anin, The Arcade, tel: 064 405 910; Die Muschel, Brauhaus Arcade, tel: 064 402 874; Stonetique, 27 Albertina Amathila Avenue, tel: 064 405 403; Hobby Horse, Brauhaus Arcade, Hendrik Witbooi Street, tel: 064 402 875; Engelhard Design, 55 Sam Nujoma Avenue, tel: 064 404 606; Karakulia, Rakotoka Street, tel: 064 461 415; Namib Stamps, Commercial Bank Arcade, Sam Nujoma Avenue, tel: 064 405 560; Peter's Antiques, 24 Tobias Hainyeko Street, tel: 064 405 624; African Leather Creations (previously Swakopmund Tannery), 22 Rakotoka Street, tel: 064 402 633.

Swakopmund Museum, Strand Street, tel: 064 402 046.

WALVIS BAY	J	F	M	A	M	J	J	A	S	O	N	D
AVERAGE TEMP. °F	63	64	63	60	60	59	55	55	55	57	60	63
AVERAGE TEMP. °C	17	18	17	16	16	15	13	13	13	14	15	17
SEA TEMP. °F	68	66	64	63	63	59	59	59	59	59	61	61
SEA TEMP. °C	20	19	18	17	17	15	15	15	15	15	16	16
RAINFALL in	0	0	0	0	0	0	0	0	0	0	0	0
RAINFALL mm	1	1	7	1	0	3	0	0	0	0	0	0
DAYS OF RAINFALL	1	1	1	1	0	1	0	0	1	0	1	0
DAYS OF MIST/FOG	8	8	11	16	16	12	15	15	12	9	9	8

5
Skeleton Coast and Kaokoveld

Situated in the remote northwestern corner of Namibia, the **Skeleton Coast** and the adjoining Kaokoveld are among the most scenic areas of southern Africa. The barren, windswept coast is often shrouded in mist for days on end, and early mariners feared this area which earned itself the reputation of being the world's largest shipping graveyard. It is a world of intricately patterned sand dunes, shimmering saltpans and plains stretching into the distance, and the habitat of a fascinating variety of animals and plants.

Adjoining the Skeleton Coast is **Kaokoland**, a region renowned for its rugged scenery and one of the world's last wilderness areas. It is the home of the Himba and a sanctuary to desert-dwelling elephant and black rhino.

South of Kaokoland lies **Damaraland**, a land of stark contrasts ranging from high mountains to rolling grasslands and plains littered with rock. This inhospitable region has many rewards for those who are prepared to tolerate excessive temperatures and bumpy roads. Not only is the **Brandberg** Namibia's highest mountain, but it is also rich in rock paintings, including the renowned White Lady. Another open-air art gallery can be viewed at **Twyfelfontein,** which is considered to be one of the largest collections of rock engravings in Africa.

The **National West Coast Recreation Area**, a 200km (124-mile) stretch of coast north of Swakopmund, is an angler's paradise, attracting fishermen from afar. Here some of the most extensive lichen fields in the world are found, and the rare Damara tern has its breeding nests.

CLIMATE

The **coast** is often blanketed in **fog**, mostly in winter. Summers are sunny, although the annual average temperature is only 16°C (61°F). Rain is rare, with a mean of about 16mm (0.6in) a year.

Summer highs of up to 40°C (104°F) are recorded in the **Kaokoveld**. Winter days are warm, but evenings are chilly and the east **wind** brings higher temperatures. The annual summer rainfall is erratic, usually less than 100mm (4in).

Opposite: *Kaokoland is one of the last remaining wilderness areas in Southern Africa.*

NATIONAL WEST COAST RECREATION AREA

This 200km (124-mile) stretch of the Namib coast between the Swakop and Ugab rivers is one of the most popular **angling areas** – indeed, the prime angling destination – in southern Africa, and it attracts thou-sands of fishing enthusiasts each year.

Galjoen, a species favouring gullies, reefs and rocky areas, is one of the most popular light-tackle fish, and there is a limit of eight per bona fide angler. Other pop-ular angling species include kob, or kabeljou, white steenbras and blacktail. To ensure that Namibia's rock and surf species are not over-exploited, angling regula-tions are strictly enforced and fishermen must ensure that they are familiar with them. Contact the Ministry of Fisheries and Marine Resources for more information.

There are several camp sites along the coast, most of them named rather unimaginatively after their distance in miles from Swakopmund. However, except for **Mile Four** just outside the town (which has bungalows, caravan and camping sites, ablution facilities and com-munal kitchens, freezers and a laundry), camping facilities are all quite basic and are used mainly by fishermen. For reservations and information contact Namibia Wildlife Resorts in Windhoek.

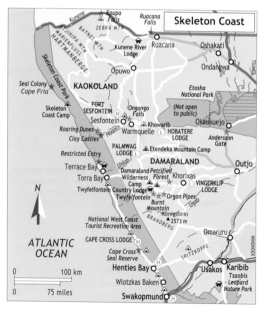

The small fishing settle-ment of **Wlotzkas Baken** is about 30km (18.5 miles) north of Swakopmund. However, the houses here are all privately owned, and the village has no tourist facilities at all.

Henties Bay, the only town along this stretch of coast, is about 75km (47

Left: *The Cape Cross Seal Reserve is home to thousands of these marine mammals, and to great numbers of Cape cormorants.*

miles) north of Swakopmund. From its humble beginnings of a few fishermen's shacks in the 1930s it has expanded into one of Namibia's prime holiday resorts. Facilities in the town include a hotel, several shops and filling stations and a rather novel nine-hole golf course which has grass greens but sand fairways.

Cape Cross Seal Reserve **

The **Cape Cross Seal Reserve**, about 120km (74.5 miles) north of Swakopmund, is one of 16 breeding colonies of the Cape fur seal along the Namibian coast.

Nearly 75% of Namibia's estimated 700,000 Cape fur seals can be found south of Hollam's Bird Island, which is about 200km (124 miles) south of Walvis Bay. At Cape Cross the seal population fluctuates between an estimated 80,000 and 260,000.

The sanctuary is open to the public daily from 10:00 to 17:00. With permit in hand (obtainable from the office at the reserve), you can observe the seals at close quarters from behind a wall.

Also of interest here is an authentic replica of the stone cross or **padrão** erected by Diego Cão, the first European to set foot on Namibian soil, in 1486. To the left of the *padrão* is a granite replica which was put here on the orders of Kaiser Wilhelm after the original was removed to Germany in 1893.

A FRAGILE ECOLOGY

Off-road driving in the Namib poses a threat to the **lichen fields** – the most extensive in the world – and the **Damara tern**, a visitor from West Africa that arrives in September and October to breed along the coast. The birds are small, grey and white, and have a black cap, make their nests up to 5km (3 miles) inland on the gravel plains and between the dunes, and lay one egg. The coast of the Namib is the summer home of up to 14,000 of these rare birds. The Namib's wide variety of more than 100 fascinating species of lichen ranges from the wind-blown types resembling bits of dead plant material to the orange tufts of the *Teloschistes*. The key to the survival of these colourful and intriguing plants is the fog which blankets the coast for more than 100 days a year.

Below: *The sunset grandeur of Spitzkoppe, inland from the Skeleton Coast. The region of Damaraland is renowned for its San rock art.*

DAMARALAND

Adjacent to the National West Coast Recreation Area lies Damaraland with its majestic flat-topped mountains, spectacular gorges, wide open plains and art treasures inherited from the earlier inhabitants.

Spitzkoppe

This imposing granite rock formation is a familiar landmark north of the road between Usakos (51km/32 miles away) and Swakopmund (180km/112 miles away). Towering some 700m (2296ft) above the surrounding plains, the sharply pointed *inselberg* is known as the **Groot Spitzkoppe**. From a distance the dome-shaped granite outcrops flanking the Groot (or large) Spitzkoppe resemble traditional African huts, hence the Afrikaans name *Pondok* (meaning grass hut). Just 15km (9 miles) to the west are the Klein (or small) Spitzkoppe.

A chain at the eastern end of the Pondok Mountains helps visitors to scramble up the steep rock to **Bushman's Paradise** – a small basin tucked away between the domes. Compared to the sparsely vegetated surrounding plains, this amphitheatre is indeed a paradise and the rock art in the overhang is testimony to the people who

once sheltered here. The paintings have been vandalized, but the overhang is still worth a visit.

There are a number of camp sites, sheltered by massive boulders, around the base of the Spitzkoppe; traditional Damara huts can also be hired on a first come, first served basis. Fireplaces, refuse bins and basic ablution facilities are provided.

Above: *Namibia's diverse regions support a variety of reptiles. The rock monitor, or leguaan, has a powerful muscular tail that it uses for self-defence.*

Brandberg

The steep slopes of this forbidding mountain, located about 170km (106 miles) west of Omaruru, are littered with gigantic granite boulders which are transformed into a glowing reddish-orange colour in the rays of the setting sun. This, combined with the dark basalt at the base, gave rise to its descriptive name, **Brandberg**, which means 'burning mountain'.

It has one of the richest collections of rock paintings in the world (more than 43,000), best known of which is the famous **White Lady** frieze. The painting was executed in an overhang in the Tsisab Ravine on the northeastern side of the mountain and was 'discovered' in 1917.

The **Brandberg (Daureb) mountain guides** offer guided walks to the White Lady frieze as well as other nearby rock painting sites, and will also provide an insight into the flora and fauna of the mountain. They are based at the Tsisab Ravine parking area. Owing to the midday heat, walks are best undertaken early in the morning and you should allow about four hours there and back. Carry at least two litres (about four pints) of water and wear a sun hat and comfortable footwear.

Bungalows, a restaurant and shady camp sites are available at the nearby Brandberg White Lady Lodge.

THE WHITE LADY

The 'White Lady Procession' was discovered in 1917, but attracted worldwide attention only after several works were published in the late 1950s by the French prehistorian, the Abbé Henri Breuil. He immediately 'identified' the central figure as a white female with Mediterranean features. Subsequently, however, the race and sex of the figure were increasingly questioned and it is now generally accepted that the White Lady is neither white, nor female. The figure displays the physical characteristics of a male carrying a bow and arrow, while the pale colour is now believed to represent body paint.

HARALD PAGER

Covering some 600km² (232 sq miles), the Brandberg has one of the richest collections of rock paintings in the world. Painted in rock overhangs, in caves and on boulders by San *shamans*, or medicine men, is an open-air art gallery unrivalled in Africa. Between 1977 and 1985 approximately 43,000 individual paintings located at 879 rock art sites were meticulously traced and recorded by the late Harald Pager. The total length of the foil used for the tracings amounted to about 6km (nearly 4 miles).

The Brandberg is Namibia's highest mountain, and the peak **Königstein**, at 2579m (8461ft) the highest point in the country, is a formidable challenge. The rugged terrain, scarcity of water and very high temperatures restrict this demanding expedition to fit and experienced hikers only. At least four days are required for a return trip to Namibia's highest peak.

Khorixas

Although the administrative centre of the Kunene region, Khorixas is a rather uninspiring, dusty town with little to offer the tourist. However, there are many attractions in the vicinity worth exploring and the **Khorixas rest camp** on the outskirts serves as a convenient base.

Set aside a morning to visit Twyfelfontein, the Petrified Forest, and the Burnt Mountain. Make an early start because of the hot temperatures at midday.

Petrified Forest

The turnoff to the **Petrified Forest** is signposted about 43km (27 miles) west of the town. These trees were uprooted elsewhere some 200 million years ago and were

Below: *Damaraland scene. This region is mostly rugged, sometimes gentle, always beautiful.*

Left: *Some of the 2400 or more petroglyphs, or rock engravings, on view among the jumbled out- crops and boulders of the Twyfelfontein (meaning doubtful spring) area. Some of them date back about 5000 years.*

swept along by rivers in flood, covered by sediments and subsequently uncovered by erosion. Local community guides provide an insight into the area and also ensure that pieces of petrified wood are not removed. Facilities for tourists include a large picnic area (under thatch), toilets and covered parking.

Twyfelfontein ★★★
Just before Twyfelfontein is the **AbaHuab camp site**, a convenient base for visitors who are geared for camping. **Twyfelfontein** is just a few kilometres away from the camp site, and a small entrance fee is charged. Here visitors have the opportunity to view one of the largest collections of rock engravings in Africa. The engravings were chiselled painstakingly into the rock slabs littering the slopes of a low, flat-topped mountain.

Twyfelfontein was inscribed as Namibia's first World Heritage Site in 2007. There is a small interpretative centre at the entrance to the site and to ensure the preservation of the rock engravings you must be accompanied by a guide. Highlights of the short option, which takes about an hour to complete, include the famous Twyfelfontein elephant, a rhinoceros with spoor instead of feet and the much-photographed lion panel. The longer route takes about 90 minutes and you will no doubt be intrigued by the 'Dancing Kudu', which is

---

TWYFELFONTEIN ROCK ENGRAVINGS

Unidentified antelope repre- sent a quarter of the 2400 engravings recorded at Twyfelfontein, while gemsbok and springbok head the list of identifiable antelope with 67 and 34 engravings respect- ively. The other most commonly depicted identi- fiable animals are: giraffe (316), ostrich (283), zebra (175) and rhinoceros (144). In addition, 383 animal spoor are also portrayed. Nearly 15% of the engravings represent abstract patterns or relate to humans (in the form of foot- prints, handprints and so on).

surrounded by numerous geometric patterns. Other points of interest along this route are the remains of huts built by pre-colonial herders and some of the relatively few rock paintings found at Twyfelfontein. Comfortable walking shoes are essential and remember to carry sufficient water. Early mornings and late afternoons are the best times to view the engravings. **Twyfelfontein Country Lodge** and **Mowani Mountain Camp** are both close to Twyfelfontein.

Organ Pipes and Burnt Mountain
Two other well-known geological features close to Twyfelfontein are the Organ Pipes and the Burnt Mountain. The **Organ Pipes**, a distinctive series of dolerite pillars that have been exposed by erosion, can be seen in the small gorge on the left-hand side of the road leading to the **Burnt Mountain**. The flat-topped mountain derives its name from the piles of blackened limestone at its base; the chunks of black dolerite combined with the crudely shaped rocks in an amazing variety of colours create the impression that the mountain has been burnt by a fierce fire. Early morning and late afternoon are the best times to visit the mountain as the kaleidescope of colours is most impressive then.

Vingerklip (Finger Rock)
Although slightly off the beaten track, a visit to the **Vingerklip**, 75km (47 miles) east of Khorixas, is well worth the detour. The 35m (115ft) column of limestone conglomerate and the surrounding table-top mountains are relics of an earlier plateau which was subsequently eroded by the Ugab River. The formation overlooks the nearby **Vingerklip Lodge** which offers luxury accommodation.

Palmwag Lodge

The rustic reed-and-thatch **Palmwag Lodge** is an ideal base from which to explore the more remote regions of northern Damaraland. It overlooks a spring where desert-dwelling elephants sometimes quench their thirst and takes its name from the makalani palms that grow around the reed-lined spring. Facilities offered at the lodge include a small shop, a restaurant, swimming pools and a camp site.

Palmwag is at the centre of the area inhabited by the world-renowned desert-dwelling elephants and black rhino, and the possibility of seeing these rare animals is one of the main attractions of the area. However, gemsbok, springbok and giraffe are more commonly sighted.

The lodge is accessible by car, but you will need a four-wheel-drive vehicle to explore the surrounding countryside. Access is strictly controlled and do-it-yourself visitors must obtain a permit at Palmwag before venturing into the concession area. Alternatively, you can join one of the safaris offered by Palmwag Lodge and Travel Shop.

Etendeka Mountain Camp

The tented camp in the adjacent **Etendeka concession area** lies among rugged mountains. Although several species of game, including desert-dwelling elephant and black rhino, make seasonal visits to the area, the emphasis here is on the fascinating plantlife and smaller creatures, like lizards, spiders and ants, which are often overlooked. The camp is accessible by four-wheel-drive vehicle only, so guests are met at the nearby airstrip or at the veterinary fence.

> **DESERT ELEPHANTS**
>
> The desert-dwelling elephants of Damaraland and Kaokoland are not a distinct species or subspecies, but they are unique. They can go without water for up to four days; during times of drought they walk up to 60km (37 miles) from their feeding grounds to reach waterholes. Unlike other elephants, they are careful in utilizing their food resources. The key to their survival is their intimate knowledge of the harsh desert. Only a small population of the estimated 700 elephants in northwestern Namibia are found between the Hoanib and Hoarusib rivers and can be classified as truly desert-dwelling.

Opposite: *The remarkable Vingerklip (Finger Rock).*
Below: *Desert-adapted elephants in Kaokoland.*

Khowarib Schlucht

The **Khowarib Schlucht Community Tourist Camp**, 76km (46 miles) north of Palmwag, on the banks of the Hoanib River, is an oasis in this arid region as here water from a spring flows in the otherwise dry river. Accommodation ranges from camp sites on the river-bank to traditional Damara and Himba huts on the high terrace overlooking the Hoanib. The camp is one of several tourism ventures in Damaraland initiated to enable the local people to share in the benefits of tourism. Visitors must be completely self-sufficient.

Warmquelle, Ongongo and Sesfontein

The small settlement of **Warmquelle**, 17km (11 miles) east of Sesfontein, is named after the lukewarm thermal spring, surrounded by shade-giving trees, that rises here. Nearby the **Ongongo Falls**, which cascades into a crystal-clear pool, invites the hot and weary traveller to cool off after a hot day's drive through the Kaokoveld. Basic camp sites as well as picnic facilities for day visitors are available. At **Sesfontein**, which takes its name from the springs surfacing here, visitors can overnight in the historic Fort Sesfontein which has been beautifully restored, with restaurant, swimming pool and camp sites.

HISTORY OF SESFONTEIN

Sesfontein derives its name from the Nama word *nanious*, which means 'six fountains'. Following the outbreak of cattle plague in 1896, a post was established here by the German colonial administration in order to control the movement of livestock. Later, the post was used to control poaching and the smuggling of firearms and ammunition to Angola.

A military station was built at Sesfontein in 1902, and in 1905–6 the building was converted to a fort. The military post was closed in 1909, but three police officers were stationed here until the police station was closed five years later.

Hobatere Lodge

Bordering Etosha, Damaraland and Kaokoland, and 80km (50 miles) from Kamanjab, **Hobatere Lodge** is an ideal stopover for the visitor on a safari into Kaokoland. The 35,000ha (86,487-acre) Hobatere Game Park is a sanctuary to a wide variety of game including lion, elephant, springbok and Hartmann's mountain zebra, as well as about 177 bird species. Accommodation at the lodge, which is surrounded by spectacular granite hills, is provided in comfortable thatched rondavels with en-suite facilities. The lodge also has a restaurant, an open-air *boma*, swimming pool and camp sites. Game and night drives, as well as guided walks, are conducted.

Skeleton Coast Park

Covering approximately 1,600,000ha (3,953,683 acres), the **Skeleton Coast Park** stretches from the Ugab River northward along the coast to the Kunene River and about 40km (25 miles) inland. It is a solitary landscape of gravel plains, sand dunes and canyons. The southern zone is accessible to tourists, while the northern zone is managed as a wilderness area.

Southern Section **

The southern section of the park is accessible along the coastal road via the Ugab River gate in the south or through the Springbokwasser gate in the east. It is an angler's paradise that attracts thousands of hopeful fishermen every year. The most popular catches are galjoen and kabeljou, while white steenbras and sea barbel are also caught.

The camp site at **Torra Bay** is closed for 10 months of the year, but in the summer months of December and January it is packed with angling enthusiasts. At **Terrace Bay**, formerly a diamond mining settlement, accommodation is provided in bungalows which once housed miners and is inclusive of three meals a day. Contact Namibia Wildlife Resorts in Windhoek for reservations and information.

ATTRACTIONS OF THE SKELETON COAST PARK

Some of the attractions in the northern **concession** area of the park are the **Clay Castles** of the Hoarusib (large silt deposits eroded into strange shapes) and the **roaring dunes**, which reverberate when large volumes of sand are displaced. Along the coast, beams and flotsam are testimony to the numerous **ships** that have run aground here, and thousands of seals crowd the beach at **Cape Frio**. In the interior, cream sand dunes and black dolerite pebbles create wonderful **abstract patterns**. The area is sparsely populated by gemsbok, springbok and ostriches, but in the Hoanib River valley you might just see the world's most fascinating elephants, the **desert-dwelling elephants** of the Namib (see page 85).

Left: *The forbidding entrance to the Skeleton Coast park at Ugab.*

Right: *The bone-dry bed of the Ugab River, venue for a challenging hiking trail.*

SHIPWRECKS

More than 100 vessels have run aground along the Skeleton Coast since the first Portuguese navigators visited Namibian shores five centuries ago. The most famous shipwreck was that of the *Dunedin Star* which ran aground north of Angra Fria in 1942. During the attempts to rescue the 21 passengers and 85 crew, one of the rescue vessels ran aground with the loss of two lives. Some of the castaways were transferred to other vessels, while others were evacuated by air from Rocky Point. The last of the survivors were transported overland and arrived in Windhoek 26 days later.

For those who would like to explore some of the scenic attractions on foot there is the **Uniab Delta Walk**, which takes two to three hours to complete. One of the highlights of the route is a spectacular waterfall which plunges into a narrow pink gorge.

Another option for the energetic is the three-day **Ugab Hiking Trail,** conducted in the Ugab River valley, on the second and fourth Thursday of every month from April to October. The hike alternates between windswept plains and the rugged river valley with its spectacular folded layers of schist, dolomite and marble. Groups are guided by a conservation official who will point out the interesting facets of the area. Hikers should be fit as they must carry all their equipment and food; nights are spent camping under the stars. Contact Namibia Wildlife Resorts in Windhoek for reservations and information.

Northern Section ✱✱✱

The northern sector of the park between the Hoanib and the Kunene rivers covers 800,000ha (1,976,841 acres) and is managed as a wilderness area. Because of the very fragile ecology and isolation of the region, access is restricted to a concession area between the Hoarusib and Nadas rivers; visitors can explore this part of the park only by joining a **fly-in** safari operated by Wilderness Safaris Namibia.

KAOKOLAND

East of the Skeleton Coast Park lies a very rugged area that is nevertheless one of Namibia's most scenic regions – **Kaokoland**. It is a starkly beautiful landscape of table-top mountains, cone-shaped hills and rock-strewn plains where desert-dwelling elephant, rhino and giraffe roam. The region is also the home of the nomadic Himba, who migrate seasonally with their herds of livestock in search of grazing, much as they did a century ago.

Covering some 49,500km² (19,112 sq miles), Kaokoland stretches from the Hoanib River northward to the Kunene. Among its scenic attractions are the **Kunene River** with the renowned **Epupa** and **Ruacana** falls, as well as the rapids at **Enyandi** and **Ondorusu**. Other interesting features of the landscape include **Marienfluss**, an extensive plain over 50km (31 miles) long, and the adjacent **Hartmann Valley**, as well as the rugged **Otjihipa**, **Baynes** and **Zebra** mountains.

The roads in this large, sparsely populated area are no more than tracks, negotiable by four-wheel-drive

---

THE HIMBA OF KAOKOLAND

The glowing, russet-coloured skin of the Himba women and the striking stature of the men are characteristics of these traditional people that will make a lasting impression on you. **Purros** is one of the best-known semipermanent Himba settlements, although small groups of dome-shaped homes are dotted throughout the area. These often give the appearance of being abandoned as the Himba are nomadic pastoralists, and when natural resources are depleted they are forced to move on with their long-horned cattle. The Himba are closely related to the other Herero-speaking people who also live in Kaokoland.

The **Ngatutunge Pamwe camp site** near Purros offers visitors overnight accommodation at a few shaded and secluded sites.

Left: *Himba women, Kaokoland.*

Right: *The perennial Kunene River's spectacular Epupa Falls in northern Kaokoland. The remote Kunene area is scenically beautiful and still untamed (although poaching reduced the numbers of wild animals in the region in the early 1980s). The main fall at Epupa plunges 36m (118ft) into a narrow gorge, but there are numerous smaller falls and cascades.*

EPUPA AND RUACANA FALLS

The **Epupa Falls**, about 190km (118 miles) upstream of the Kunene River mouth, is one of Kaokoland's most breathtaking sights. Here the river fans out into a number of channels before cascading into a deep gorge. There are plans to build Namibia's second hydro-electric scheme downstream of Epupa, but no date has been set yet for the start of the project.

The well-known **Ruacana Falls**, about 120km (74.5 miles) upstream, is dry for most of the year, but after good rains the Kunene becomes a seething, thundering mass of water that tumbles into the 120m (394ft) deep gorge.

vehicles only. Always travel in a party of at least two vehicles to safeguard against being stranded in the event of a breakdown as it could take several days before another vehicle passes in this remote area. To get the most out of a visit to Kaokoland, you should plan to spend at least five days in the region, and make sure that you are well equipped and prepared (firewood, fresh water, ample fuel supplies, a mosquito net and anti-malaria medication are essential).

Opuwo, the administrative centre of the area, is a frontier town in the true sense of the word. It does not have any tourist attractions, but is the only settlement in the region where fuel and a limited supply of groceries can be purchased.

Several tour operators offer guided safaris into Kaokoland; if you are unfamiliar with the area, your best option is to join one of these.

Skeleton Coast and Kaokoveld at a Glance

BEST TIMES TO VISIT

Along the **coast**, moderate temperatures but windy and misty year-round. Rain is rare. **November** to **March** best for angling. **Inland**, cooler months **May** to **August** best. High temperatures and flash floods in summer. Most rain between January and March.

GETTING THERE

Air Namibia, tel: 061 299 6444, fax: 299 6168, has several scheduled weekly flights from Windhoek to Walvis Bay. **Landing strips** at Henties Bay, Mile 108, Torra Bay and Terrace Bay, and near Palmwag, Etendeka, Hobatere and Epupa; contact (Windhoek) Desert Air, tel: 061 228 101, fax: 248 316; Comav, tel: 061 227 512; Westair, tel: 061 221 091, fax: 232 778; (Swakopmund) Pleasure Flights, tel/fax: 064 404 500.

GETTING AROUND

Roads on **Skeleton Coast** accessible by car; four-wheel-drive needed to go off the beaten track for angling. **Car and four-wheel-drive hire** in Swakopmund (*see* page 74). **Khorixas** accessible by tarred road via Outjo. Attractions in **Damaraland** reached by gravel-surface roads, accessible by car but conditions vary. Party of at least two four-wheel-drives essential in **Kaokoland** as roads not sign-posted and often mere tracks.

WHERE TO STAY

National West Coast Recreation Area
Mile 4 camp site: tel: 064 461 781.
Hotel De Duine, Henties Bay: tel: 061 374 750.
Cape Cross Lodge at Cape Cross: Luxury rooms, tel: 064 694 012, fax: 694 013.

Kaokoland
Kunene River Lodge, tel: 061 237 294, fax: 237 295.

Damaraland
Etendeka Mountain Camp: tel: 061 226 979, fax: 226 999.
Hobatere Lodge, Kamanjab: tel: 067 687 066, fax: 687 067.
Damaraland Camp: tel: 061 274 500.
Mowani Mountain Camp: tel: 061 232 009, fax: 222 574.
Palmwag Lodge: tel: 064 416 820, fax: 404 664.
Twyfelfontein Country Lodge: tel: 061 374 750, fax: 256 598.

WHERE TO EAT

National West Coast Recreation Area
Spitzkoppe Restaurant, Henties Bay: seafood and steaks, tel: 064 500 394.
De Duine Hotel Restaurant, Henties Bay, tel: 064 500 001.

Damaraland
Restaurants at **Khorixas**, **Palmwag** and **Fort Sesfontein**.

TOURS AND EXCURSIONS

Namibia Tracks & Trails offers **tours** of **Damaraland** from camps situated at Palmwag and on the Kunene River, tel: 064 416 820, fax: 404 664. Kaokohimba Safaris specializes in overland and fly-in **safaris** to **Damaraland**, **Kaokoland** and the Kunene River, tel: 065 685 021. Contact Safari Adventure Co. to arrange **fly-in safaris** to the concession area in the Skeleton Coast Park, tel: 061 274 500, fax: 239 455. For **canoeing** on the **Kunene River**, contact Kunene River Lodge, tel: 061 237 294, fax: 237 295.

USEFUL TELEPHONE NUMBERS

Ministry of Fisheries and Marine Resources, tel: 064 410 1000.
Namibia Wildlife Resorts, Swakopmund, tel: 064 402 172.

SKELETON COAST	J	F	M	A	M	J	J	A	S	O	N	D
AVERAGE TEMP. °F	66	66	66	63	61	59	57	55	57	59	61	64
AVERAGE TEMP. °C	19	19	19	17	16	15	14	13	14	15	16	18
RAINFALL in	0	0	0.5	0	0	0	0	0	0	0	0	0
RAINFALL mm	3	3	0	1	0	0	0	0	0	0	0	0
DAYS OF RAINFALL	1	1	1	1	0	0	0	0	0	0	0	0

6
Etosha and
the North

Etosha, the Great White Place, is regarded as one of the world's great game parks and is Namibia's prime tourist attraction. It is the home of several rare and endangered species of game, including one of the largest populations of black rhino in the world, as well as thousands of antelope. Situated a mere five hours' drive from Windhoek, the park is easily accessible from the capital and a visit can be combined with sightseeing of the numerous other tourist attractions in the area.

Long before people started roaming across the ancient landscape, dinosaurs left their footprints in the mud of what used to be an enormous lake. Evidence of these prehistoric reptiles can be seen northeast of **Omaruru**, while the fossilized remains of a prehuman hominid dating back some 13 million years were discovered in the **Otavi Mountains**. In more recent historical times the last of the Stone Age hunter–gatherers, the San, adorned the walls of the overhangs in the **Erongo Mountain** with delicate rock paintings.

The **Waterberg Plateau Park** with its sheer cliffs is a natural sanctuary to several rare and endangered species of game that can be viewed on a hiking trail or by joining a tour on an open safari vehicle. Other well-known attractions of this region include the **Hoba Meteorite** near **Grootfontein** and **Lake Otjikoto**, an enormous sinkhole near Tsumeb.

The area north of Etosha, formerly known as **Owamboland**, has much potential as a tourist destination, but is mainly used as a transit route to northern Kaokoland.

CLIMATE

The **dry winter** months are the best time to visit the region. Early mornings and evenings are cool, with minimum temperatures of below 5°C (41°F) being recorded at Grootfontein, but daytime temperatures are moderate. Stifling **summer** temperatures of over 30°C (86°F) are common, and **humidity** is often high. Most of the region's **rainfall**, which ranges from 350mm (14in) to 570mm (22in), is recorded between December and April. Heavy showers are accompanied by **thunderstorms**, usually in the mid-afternoon.

Opposite: *A magnificent elephant at Etosha.*

THE ERONGOS

The Erongo Mountain, a roughly circular massif, dominates the flat plains west of Omaruru and gives the **Erongo region** its name. The mountain is an eroded relic of a volcano that was active 140 million years ago.

The most notable rock painting here is the **'White Elephant'** frieze in **Phillip's Cave** on the southern edge of the mountain, situated on the farm **Ameib**, 30km (19 miles) from Usakos and 240km (150 miles) from Windhoek. It is a 45-minute walk each way to view the painting, but the scenery makes the ramble worthwhile. Fascinating rock formations such as the **Elephant Head** and the **Bull's Party** are also an attraction here. Ameib is open to visitors from sunrise to sunset; an entrance fee is charged. The guest farm also offers a variety of accommodation, from camp sites to en-suite rooms.

Omaruru is a pleasant country town built on the banks of the river of that name that developed around the Rhenish mission established here in 1868. Reminders

THE HERERO OF OMARURU

The history of Omaruru is closely linked to that of the Herero nation, and the town is the seat of the western Herero who settled here in the 1830s under their Chief Zeraua. A colourful **procession** is held through the streets of the town in October each year when members of the Zeraua chiefdom, also known as the 'White Flag' Herero, pay tribute to their leaders. The **Franke Tower** and the adjacent battlefield are a reminder of the Uprising of 1904, which spread to Omaruru on 17 January 1904 when the Herero besieged the town. The siege was relieved 20 days later by Captain Victor Franke after a fierce eight-hour battle. The stone tower was erected in 1908 to commemorate the relief of Omaruru.

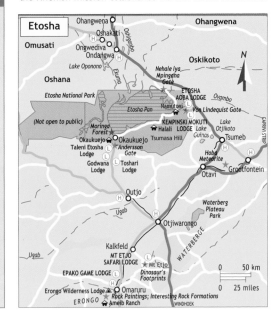

of its early history include the **Rhenish Mission House** in Wilhelm Zeraua Street, built in 1871, which serves as a museum, and the nearby **Rhenish Mission Church**, completed in 1872. Displays in the museum include photographs of the early missionaries, old furniture and farming implements. Contact the municipality (in Wilhelm Zeraua Street, tel: 064 570 028) in advance to arrange a visit to the museum during weekdays.

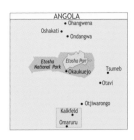

From Kalkfeld, 68km (42 miles) north of Omaruru, it is a 32km (20-mile) detour to the **Dinosaur Tracks**, a national monument, on the farm **Otjihaenamaperero**. An entrance fee is charged to visit the site, sunrise to sunset daily. From the parking area it is about a 10-minute walk to the sloping rock slab where the footprints of a three-toed dinosaur were deeply imbedded into the sandstone Etjo formation some 150 to 185 million years ago. Camp sites and picnic places for day visitors are available.

One of Namibia's oldest and best-known game lodges, **Mount Etjo Safari Lodge**, is situated about 34km (21 miles) east of Kalkfeld. It is named after the Etjo Mountain, a flat-topped massif, capped by sandstone of the Etjo Formation, which has resisted erosion. Accommodation is provided in luxury en-suite rooms and there is an inviting swimming pool with a pool bar. Dinner is served in a *boma*. Activities include early-morning and late-afternoon game drives and guided walks. The numerous animals roaming the nature reserve include both white and black rhino, elephant and a variety of antelope. Of special interest are the lion feeds that can be viewed from the safety and comfort of a hide every evening.

The visitor and education centre of the **Cheetah Conservation Fund** (CCF), 44km (27 miles) northeast of Otjiwarongo, provides a fascinating insight into various aspects of the world's fastest land mammal, the cheetah. Visitors can watch the

Below: *The historic Franke Tower at Omaruru, an attractively embowered centre of a cattle and dairy farming region, was built in 1908 and declared a national monument in 1963. In front of the tower stands the cannon used during the battle to relieve the siege of Omaruru.*

cheetahs being fed at around 14:00 Mondays to Fridays and around noon on Saturdays and Sundays (tel: 067 306 225 to confirm times). The work of the CCF is aimed at ensuring the long-term survival of the cheetah through research, education and conservation programmes.

Above: *The pleasant pool area at the Waterberg Plateau's rest camp.*
Opposite: *The mining town of Tsumeb.*

WATERBERG TRAILS

Guided wilderness trails are conducted from a base camp in the 18,000ha (44,480-acre) wilderness area on the plateau on the second, third and fourth weekend of each month, from April through to November. Groups of six to eight people are led by an armed ranger. Trailists must bring their own food, but all other equipment is provided.

From April to November groups of 3–10 can undertake a four-day **self-guided hiking trail** covering 42km (26 miles). Trailists must be self-sufficient in all respects and, since tone can encounter potentially dangerous animals such as rhino and buffalo, hikers must be alert, fit and able to take evasive action fast.

THE WATERBERG PLATEAU PARK

Rising approximately 200m (656ft) above the surrounding plains, the Waterberg Plateau with its impressive steep-sided cliffs is also en route to Etosha. The plateau was declared a game park in 1972, and is a sanctuary to an interesting variety of game, including black and white rhino, buffalo, roan and sable antelope, as well as more common species such as giraffe, kudu, red hartebeest and eland.

Although visitors are not allowed to explore the plateau in their own vehicles, guided **game-viewing tours** are conducted every morning and afternoon. A guided **wilderness trail** and self-guided **hiking trail** are also offered, and short walks have been laid out in the rest camp, one of which leads to the top of the plateau.

The cliffs of the Waterberg are the habitat of Namibia's only breeding population of Cape vultures. Sadly, their numbers have decreased from about 500 in the late 1950s to just a few birds.

Amenities at the pleasant **Waterberg Camp**, which was built to blend in with the surroundings, include the historic *Rasthaus* restaurant, a shop, a filling station and a swimming pool.

Further along the B1 to Etosha is the first town north of Okahandja, **Otjiwarongo**. Of interest here is the **crocodile ranch**, started in 1985. Crocodiles are bred for their skins, which are exported to Europe where they are much in demand for the manufacture of high-quality shoes and handbags. Visitors are shown around the ranch, which is open Mondays to Fridays 09:00 to 16:00, Saturdays 08:00 to 13:00, and Sundays and public holidays 09:00 to 14:00. Times differ slightly in winter.

From Otjiwarongo, the B1 leads to Otavi, Tsumeb, Namutoni in Etosha and Oshakati; the C38 gives visitors access to Damaraland and Okaukuejo in Etosha, via Outjo. On the former route a signpost about 28km (17 miles) west of Grootfontein shows the way to the **Hoba Meteorite**. The well-known attraction is about 24km (15 miles) further on along a gravel-surface road.

Grootfontein with its tree-lined streets is one of the largest towns in the north of the country and an important farming centre. Its Afrikaans name means 'large fountain' and refers to the strong springs in Tree Park. The **museum** in the historic fort off Eriksson Street has a collection of photographs depicting the history of the area, a fine collection of rocks and gems, and a display on wagon and cart manufacturing. It is open on weekdays from 08:30 to 16:30, but times could differ slightly in winter. Weekend viewing for groups of six or more is by arrangement.

Known as 'The Gateway to Etosha', **Tsumeb** was established in 1905 by the Otavi Minen und Eisenbahn Gesellschaft (OMEG) and most of the places of interest in Tsumeb reflect the town's close links with the development of the mining industry. Buildings from this era include the **Second Director's House** in Hospital Street, the nearby **Omeg Minenbüro**, dating back to 1907, and **St Barbara's Catholic Church** in Main Road, which was built in 1913 and named after the Patron Saint of Miners.

Until its closure in

HOBA METEORITE

With an estimated weight of 60 tonnes, the Hoba meteorite is the largest in the world. It measures 2.95m (9.7ft) by 2.84m (9.3ft) across, and its thickness varies between 122cm (48in) and 75cm (29.5in). It consists of 82.4% iron, 16.4% nickel and 0.76% cobalt, and traces of carbon, sulphur, chromium, copper and other elements. The age of the meteorite has been estimated at between 410 and 190 million years, but indications are that it fell to the earth less than 80,000 years ago.

Above: *The mysterious Lake Otjikoto, near Etosha, is actually a large sinkhole. The waters are home to the unique Otjikoto tilapia.*

late 1997, the Tsumeb Mine was a major producer of copper and lead, while silver, cadmium, zinc and arsenic trioxide were produced as by-products. The smelter produces blister copper and refined lead from other mines.

The **Tsumeb Museum** in Main Street is housed in the old German school and exhibits minerals from the Tsumeb Mine. There is an excellent collection of armaments abandoned by the German forces in Lake Otjikoto in 1915 – some of the items on display are several beautifully restored cannons, ammunition carriers and machine guns. Open from 09:00 to 12:00 and 14:00 to 17:00 on weekdays, and 09:00 to 12:00 on Saturdays (times could differ slightly in winter).

About 24km (15 miles) from Tsumeb is another well-known tourist attraction, **Lake Otjikoto**. The lake is a sinkhole formed by underground water that dissolved the dolomite rock to form a huge cavern, the roof of which subsequently collapsed.

The endangered ***Otjikoto tilapia*** is found here and in only one other place, the nearby Lake Guinas. This species reaches a length of up to 14cm (5.5in) and varies in colour from dark greenish-black to a combination of white, black, yellow and blue.

In 1915 the retreating German forces dumped their armaments in the lake rather than let them fall in the hands of the advancing South African forces. Several of the armaments have been recovered and are on display in the Khorab Room at the Tsumeb Museum.

Another sunken lake, **Guinas**, is situated southwest of Otjikoto, but since it is a 50km (31-mile) return trip from the main road, it is usually bypassed. Visitors with time on hand will find the detour rewarding as Guinas is not only deeper than Otjikoto but it is also far more scenic.

RICHES FROM THE EARTH

The Tsumeb ore body was formed 600 million years ago when a bewildering variety of minerals were injected into an underground cavity. Forty of the 213 minerals contained in the ore body were found only at Tsumeb. The mine was renowned for its magnificent specimens of secondary copper minerals such as azurite and dioptase, and spectacular crystals of mimetite and wulfenite. Some fine specimens of minerals from the mine are displayed in the **Tsumeb Museum** in Main Street, but unfortunately the most comprehensive collection is in the Smithsonian Institute Museum of Natural History in Washington.

Etosha National Park

Centred on the vast Etosha Pan with its shimmering mirages, the renowned Etosha National Park is one of the world's greatest conservation areas. It is a sanctuary to large herds of animals typical of the African plains, and entices tourists hoping to spot four of the 'big five' – lion, elephant, leopard and rhino. After the summer rains thousands of waterbirds are attracted to the seasonally inundated pans and vleis.

Covering 22,270km² (8,598 sq miles), Etosha stretches for about 300km (186 miles) from west to east and 110km (68 miles) from north to south at its widest point.

The western part of the park has not been developed for tourism and as the animals are not used to vehicles, species such as lions and elephants tend to be aggressive. Tourists cannot visit this section of the park individually, only with a tour operator registered by the Ministry of Environment and Tourism.

Entry permits are necessary. There are three entrance gates to the park: Von Lindequist near Namutoni, Andersson near Okaukuejo, and Nehale lya Mpingana on the northern boundary near Andoni Waterhole.

Warning: Only leave your vehicle in designated places, and keep a respectful distance from elephants, especially lone bulls and cows with calves. Never feed wild animals and do not sleep in the open in rest camps.

Etosha Pan

The white clay pan covers about 5000 km² (1930.5 sq miles), or nearly 25% of the park's surface. It is often dry for decades, but the flood waters of the Ekuma and Oshigambo rivers in the north and the Owambo River in the east occasionally inundate the pan, creating a vast, shallow inland lake. Although the salinity of the water is twice as high as that of sea water, the shallow water creates ideal conditions for the growth of blue-green algae, which provides a feeding ground for up to a million flamingoes in years with good rains. The pan is classified as a saline desert and, with the exception of a hardy, salt-loving grass, it supports hardly any other vegetation when it is dry.

Left: *An elephant visits guests at Etosha's Okaukuejo. The camp boasts a viewing platform and a floodlit water hole.*

FORT NAMUTONI

The first fort at Namutoni, a six-room structure, was built in 1902–3. It was razed to the ground when it was attacked by Owambo warriors in January 1904. A much larger fortification was constructed in 1905, and was handed over to the Police five years later. For economic reasons it was closed in 1912, but at the beginning of World War I a military garrison was stationed at Namutoni. After the war, the South African Police occupied the fort for some time, but the building gradually fell into disrepair. The historic landmark was declared a national monument in 1950, and after it was restored according to its original plans the 'third' Fort Namutoni was opened in 1958 as tourist accommodation.

Below: *The historic fort at the Namutoni rest camp.*

Accommodation

The eastern section of the park is traversed by a network of more than 700km (435 miles) of tourist roads, and accommodation is provided in three rest camps, Okaukuejo in the west, Halali in the centre and Namutoni in the east. The accommodation ranges from thatched bungalows to rooms in the historic Fort Namutoni and camp sites. Amenities at each camp include a restaurant serving breakfast, lunch and dinner, a shop that stocks groceries, curios and liquor, a filling station and a swimming pool.

Each of the three rest camps has a distinctive atmosphere. **Okaukuejo**, 18km (11 miles) from the Andersson Gate in the south, was originally used as a Police post and is the oldest rest camp in the park. A characteristic feature of the camp is the limestone water tower, which affords stunning views of the surrounding plains. An attraction at Okaukuejo is the floodlit water hole just outside the perimeter of the camp.

Halali rest camp, midway between Okaukuejo and Namutoni, is surrounded by dense mopane woodlands near Tsumasa Hill, a small dolomite outcrop. A short walk has been laid out against the hill and the view from the top is especially beautiful at sunset. The lower slopes of the hill overlook a floodlit water hole.

The central feature of **Namutoni**, just 12km (7.5 miles) from the Von Lindequist Gate in the east, is the picturesque old fort with its whitewashed walls. Here too visitors can watch the animals drinking at a water hole just outside the camp's perimeter. Contact Namibia Wildlife Resorts for accommodation in Etosha National Park.

Wildlife ★★★

Although the park is the habitat of about 114 mammal species, the average visitor is unlikely to see more than 20 species. The attraction of Etosha is not its diversity of species or large numbers of game, but the relative ease with which a variety of game can be seen, especially during the dry winter months. During the rainy season, however, the animals disperse widely throughout the park until the diminishing field water forces them to concentrate in the vicinity of the water holes.

Etosha's **lion** population has decreased from over 500 in 1981 to an estimated 190–265, but these magnificent animals are still often seen near water holes, especially during the dry winter months. **Cheetah** and **leopard** are less frequently spotted.

Elephants are commonly sighted, but their numbers fluctuate considerably as many migrate out of the park during the wet season.

Giraffe are plentiful throughout the park, while the smaller **black-backed jackal** and **ground squirrel** are also likely to be seen. **Spotted hyena** and **warthog** are two other mammals to look out for.

Etosha has the largest population of the southwestern subspecies of the black rhino in the world, totalling over

Above: *Etosha has a large resident population of lion, Africa's largest predator.*

LIONS ON THE PILL

During the early 1980s it became apparent that Etosha's exploding lion population (numbering about 500) would have to be controlled. As an alternative to culling, a unique population control experiment was conducted by implanting a slow-releasing hormonal capsule into the neck muscles of 10 lionesses. None of the treated lionesses fell pregnant, but when the contraceptives were removed, they became pregnant within 36 days. Because of a decrease in the lion population it was not necessary to put lionesses on the pill.

ETOSHA'S RARE ANIMALS

The park is a sanctuary to several rare and endangered animals, including:
• The **black-faced impala** is closely related to the impala, an antelope that is widely distributed elsewhere in southern Africa. This rare impala is easily identified by its distinctive facial blaze and its reddish-brown colour.
• With more than 800 **black rhino** Etosha has the largest population of this endangered species in the world.
• The dainty and diminutive **Damara dik-dik** is easily seen in the dense woodlands near Namutoni, often at extremely close range.

800 animals. They are often seen at the floodlit water hole at Okaukuejo, as well as in the Halali area. **White rhino** were reintroduced into the park in 1995 after they became locally extinct nearly a century earlier.

Springbok are the most numerous **antelope** and during summer and early autumn they congregrate in herds of several hundred on the open plains, while several thousand gemsbok and Burchell's zebra also roam the plains. Other antelope include eland, red hartebeest and kudu, as well as steenbok and common duiker.

Although fencing the park has created a sanctuary for the animals, migratory species such as the **blue wildebeest** have been affected adversely. During the late 1950s Etosha's blue wildebeest population numbered over 25,000, but as a result of the disruption of their migration route, anthrax and competition with other plains animals, their numbers declined to fewer than 2200 in the early 1980s. Numbers now range between 3400 and 5900.

The diversity of habitats attracts a wide variety of **birds** and to date about 392 species have been recorded.

After the summer rains have set in, a number of migrants from the northern hemisphere join the resident species. Fischer's Pan near Namutoni attracts a large variety of waterbirds and in years of exceptionally good rainfall Etosha Pan attracts up to a million flamingoes. Species likely to be of interest to birders include the bare-cheeked babbler, often seen at Halali, and the black-faced babbler, recorded in the woodlands of eastern Etosha. The crowned crane may be sighted on the Andoni Plains, north of Namutoni, after summer rains, where bird-watchers should also keep an eye out for blue crane and clapper lark.

Vegetation

The **vegetation** of Etosha is dominated by mopane savanna and woodlands, while the edge of the pan is fringed by dwarf shrub savannas, except in the west where it is bordered by grassland which attracts thousands of antelope after the summer rains. Sandwiched between the dwarf shrub savannas and the mopane savanna and woodlands to the south of the pan is a narrow strip of grassland which is utilized as a winter grazing area. Several other vegetation types can also be distinguished – a few kilometres south of Namutoni the vegetation is dominated by tall, dense tamboti and purple-pod terminalia woodlands, while the vegetation of the northeastern corner of the park consists of a mixed tree and shrub savanna.

PRIVATE GAME RESERVES

In recent years a number of luxury game lodges have been opened close to the park's two entrance gates. **Onguma Game Reserve** adjoining Fischer's Pan on the eastern boundary has a diversity of game and offers a variety of accommodation.

Kempinski Mokuti Lodge, at the eastern gate to the park, is rated as one of Namibia's top hotels. Mokuti means 'in the bush' in the Owambo language, and, appropriately, the rustic, thatched bungalows blend in

---

MORINGA TREE

The hardy moringa tree, known also as the phantom tree, usually grows on rocky slopes. **Tsumasa Hill** in Halali rest camp is a typical habitat of the moringa, and here visitors can closely inspect the tree. However, at the **Moringa Forest**, west of Okaukuejo, several hundred of these trees grow on the open plains. The moringa usually has a straight, upright trunk, but those growing at the Moringa Forest are grotesquely shaped with gnarled trunks, while some have several trunks – hence this is often called the Haunted Forest or the Ghost Forest. The weird shapes of the trees have been attributed to browsing by giraffe and elephant.

Above: *Game-viewing from an open vehicle.*
Opposite: *A cuca shop in northern Namibia.*

WATER HOLES OF ETOSHA

In addition to constructed drinking places (water holes), there are three types of natural springs that provide water for the wildlife in the park. Along the edge of the pan there are several **contact springs** which are created by water seeping through the calcrete and then being forced to the surface when it reaches the underlying impermeable clay. **Water-level springs** are usually associated with limestone and are found in places where the water table is higher than the ground level. In some areas (usually on top of limestone outcrops), water is forced upwards under pressure to form **artesian springs**.

---

well with the vegetation.

Accommodation ranges from single to family and luxury units with en-suite facilities, and all units are air conditioned. Guests can view game, including giraffe, kudu and gemsbok, on foot by following self-guided walking routes, while a variety of reptiles can be seen in the **Ontouka Reptile Park**. It is open daily from sunrise to sunset. The lodge also has swimming pools, a spa, a gym and tennis courts.

Also located near the eastern gate is **Etosha Aoba Lodge**, built amidst the 7000ha (17,300-acre) **Fischer's Pan Private Game Reserve** bordering on the Etosha National Park in the west. The reserve is home to a rich diversity of game, with antelope such as blue wildebeest, kudu and springbok, as well as giraffe, leopard and hyena. Visitors are accommodated in ten thatched cottages (with en-suite facilities) shaded by tamboti trees.

A wide choice of accommodation is available outside the park close to the southern gate. Just 10km (6 miles) from Andersson Gate, **Gondwana Etosha** offers reasonably priced accommodation in the Etosha Safari Camp which has chalets, a restaurant, bar, swimming pool and camp site. The more up-market Etosha Safari Lodge has chalets, a restaurant, bar and three swimming pools.

The **Taleni Etosha Village**, just 4km (2.5 miles) from Andersson Gate, offers accommodation in self-catering tented units, each with its own outside kitchen/dining area, three restaurants, a bar, swimming pool and a shop.

At **Toshari Lodge**, 25km (15 miles) south of Andersson Gate, guests are accommodated in rooms, and there are also a few camp sites. Facilities include a restaurant and a swimming pool.

THE NORTH

North of Etosha the landscape is dominated by an exceptionally flat plain that is covered by a network of shallow watercourses, known as *oshanas*, in the central area. Formerly known as Owambo, the area has been divided into four regions: **Omusati** in the west, the central **Oshana** region, **Ohangwena** and **Oshikoto**.

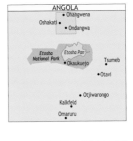

With a total population of about 650,000 people, northern Namibia is the most densely populated area in the country. About three-quarters of the people live in the rural areas where they practise crop production and livestock farming. The most important crops cultivated are millet, locally known as *mahangu*, sorghum and beans, while cattle farming is another important agricultural activity. Owambo women are skilled at basketry, and baskets, pottery and handmade musical instruments can be bought from roadside stalls in the region.

Oshakati, **Ongwediva** and **Ondangwa**, the only major towns north of Etosha, are unlike any other settlements in Namibia. They are a hive of activity with people thronging around the open-air stalls along the main roads and taxis careering along the roads at breakneck speed. Stray cattle, donkeys and goats pose a threat to motorists, so be alert, even in the towns.

Attractions include the historic Finnish mission complex at **Olukonda**, 13km south of Ondangwa. It comprises the historic mission house, the mission church dating back to 1889, the Nakambale Museum and a traditional Ndonga homestead. The accommodation ranges from a stay in this traditional Ndongwa homestead to camp sites. The gigantic **Ombalantu baobab tree** at Outapi (there are also camp sites available) and the royal homestead at Tsandi are also worth a visit.

CUCA SHOPS

A familiar feature of the north are the thousands of informal trading stores, known as *cuca* shops. The name was originally adopted by shops on the Angolan border that sold Angolan beer of that name, but is now used throughout the north. The square, tin-roofed buildings are usually painted in bright colours and are given way-out names like, 'Jamaica Inn' or 'Love Station'. Basic commodities and liquor are sold, and they close when the last customers leave.

Etosha and the North at a Glance

April to **September** is most popular – cooler temperatures are pleasant for game-viewing and hiking. Dry winter months of **May** to **September** are best for game-viewing in Etosha as animals congregate around water holes. **Summer** is best for bird-watching as numerous migrant species visit the pans after summer rains.

Air Namibia, tel: 061 299 6444, fax: 299 6168, has regular **scheduled flights** to Ondangwa. There are **landing strips** at all three rest camps in Etosha, at Mount Etjo Safari Lodge and at Epupa Falls. For **air charter** contact (Windhoek) Comav, tel: 061 227 512; Desert Air, tel: 061 228 101, fax: 248 316; Westair, tel: 061 221 091, fax: 232 778.All major towns in the region are connected to Windhoek by a **tarred road**. Intercape Mainliner, tel: 061 227 847, has a **coach** to Victoria Falls via Otavi and Grootfontein on Mondays and Fridays.

The region is served by an excellent **road network** and all tourist attractions are accessible by car (except some parts of the north). **Gravel-surface** roads usually in good condition. **Car hire** from Avis at Tsumeb, Jordan Street, tel/fax: 067 220

824; Mokuti Lodge (by prior arrangement), tel/fax: 067 220 520; Imperial-Europcar, 1551 Omeg Allee, Tsumeb, tel: 067 220 728, fax: 220 916. Further north, cars and **four-wheel-drive** vehicles can be hired from Cheetah Car Hire in Ongwediva, tel: 065 231 786, fax: 231 044. TransNamib offers three **passenger train** services a week between Windhoek/ Walvis Bay, Otjiwarongo and Tsumeb, tel: 061 298 2175.

Kalkfeld
Mount Etjo Safari Lodge, near Kalkfeld: excellent accommodation and service, guided walks, game-viewing drives and viewing of nightly lion feeds; accommodation in en-suite rooms, and the lodge has a swimming pool with a pool bar, tel: 067 290 174, fax: 290 172.

Omaruru
Ameib Ranch, foot of Erongo Mountain: offers accommodation in a farmhouse and camp sites; attractions include rock paintings in Phillip's Cave and interesting rock formations, tel: 064 530 803.

Ekapo Game Lodge, near Omaruru: offers accommodation in bungalows, game-viewing drives and walking trails, tel: 064 570 551, fax: 570 553.

Erongo Wilderness Lodge, 10km (6 miles) west of

Omaruru in Erongo Mountains: luxury tents under thatch raised on platforms, nature walks and drives, rock paintings and good birding, tel: 061 239 199, fax: 234 971.

Ondangwa
Protea Hotel Ondangwa, near centre of business district: three-star hotel, air-conditioned rooms with en-suite facilities, restaurant, bar and swimming pool, tel: 065 241 900, fax: 241 919.

Oshakati
Santorini Inn: has en-suite rooms, a restaurant and bar, tel: 065 220 457.
Oshakati Country Hotel: luxury en-suite double rooms, restaurant, bar and swimming pool, tel: 065 222 380.

Outjo
Gondwana Etosha, 10km (6 miles) from the Andersson Gate, has two accommodation options. **Etosha Safari Lodge** has chalets, a restaurant, a bar and a swimming pool.
Etosha Safari Camp offers good value for money. It has chalets, a restaurant, a bar, a swimming pool and camp sites; tel: 061 230 066, fax: 251 863.
Taleni Etosha Village, 4km (2.5 miles) from Andersson Gate, has self-catering tented units each with an outside kitchen/dining area, restaurant, bar, swimming pool and

shop, tel: +27 21 930 4564, fax: 930 4574.

Toshari Lodge, 25km (15.5 miles) south of Andersson Gate, has chalets, a restaurant, a swimming pool and camp sites, tel: 067 333 440, fax: 333 444.

Tsumeb

Kempinski Mokuti Lodge, near eastern boundary of Etosha: en-suite accommodation, restaurant, swimming pool with a pool bar, tel and fax: 061 388 400.

Etosha Aoba Lodge, near the eastern boundary of Etosha: thatched chalets, guided nature drives and walks, tel: 067 229 100, fax: 229 101.

Tariffs at all **lodges** and **guest farms** are inclusive of three meals a day. The **Onduli Dining Room** at Mokuti Lodge offers excellent buffet meals with a variety of game dishes. **Etosha National Park** offers buffet meals in the restaurants in the three rest camps.

The **Bäckerei & Café Jakob**, Okavango Street, Grootfontein has the best German confectionery in the north of the country and a tea or lunch stop is highly recommended.

In the north, **Protea Hotel Ondangwa** in Ondangwa has a restaurant, and **Santorini Inn** and the **Oshakati Country Hotel** in Oshakati both have restaurants.

Tours of Etosha National Park: Early-morning and late-afternoon game-viewing drives from Mokuti Lodge to the Etosha National Park. Etosha Fly-In Safaris, based at Tsumeb, also offers a fully inclusive fly-in service to Etosha National Park, tel: 067 220 574, fax: 220 832.

Waterberg Plateau Park: guided game-viewing tours in open four-wheel-drive vehicles are conducted twice a day; in addition, guided three-day wilderness trails are conducted weekly between April and November.

Tours of Etosha, with additional scheduled stops at Lake Otjikoto and Tsumeb, are offered by Sense of Africa, tel: 061 275 300. Safari Adventure Co., tel: 061 274 545, offers **fly-in safaris to Etosha**. If you are intending to go off and explore off-the-beaten-track destinations in the north of the country, it is advisable to purchase **topographical maps** of the area from the Surveyor General, on the corner of Robert Mugabe Avenue and Dr AB May Street, Windhoek;

the **Automobile Association** (AA), situated on the corner of Independence Avenue and Fidel Castro Street, Windhoek, tel: 061 224 201, provides travel information for members.

A variety of books showcasing the Etosha area is available at the three rest camps in the park. Here is a select list:
Etosha National Park by David Rogers; useful compact guide in full colour.
Sasol Birds of Southern Africa by Ian Sinclair; comprehensive, full-colour guide.
Field Guide to the Mammals of Southern Africa by Chris and Tilde Stuart; informative, with colour photographs.

Grootfontein Museum, tel: 067 242 456.
Namibia Wildlife Resorts, Windhoek, tel: 061 285 7200.
Museum at Omaruru, contact the municipality, tel: 064 570 028.
Namibia Tourism, Windhoek, tel: 061 290 6000, fax: 254 848.
Tsumeb Tourism Centre, tel: 067 220 728.

ETOSHA PAN	J	F	M	A	M	J	J	A	S	O	N	D
AVERAGE TEMP. °F	79	77	75	73	66	61	61	66	73	79	79	79
AVERAGE TEMP. °C	26	25	24	23	19	16	16	19	23	26	26	26
RAINFALL in	3	4	3	1	1	0	0	0	0	0	1	2.5
RAINFALL mm	75	109	75	26	18	1	0	0	2	7	31	68
DAYS OF RAINFALL	15	13	11	6	1	0	0	0	1	5	9	13

7
Kavango and Caprivi

Northeastern Namibia, with its woodlands, rivers and swamps, is unlike any other part of the country, and is usually a complete surprise to the first-time visitor.

Nyae Nyae, previously eastern Bushmanland, is home to the Ju!Wasi San (Bushmen) who have lived here for thousands of years. Do not expect to see the Bushman portrayed in coffee-table books, though; the Ju!Wasi are a people in transition, determined to control their future.

To the north lie the **Kavango** and the **Khaudum Game Park**, sanctuary to the rare roan antelope, the endangered wild dog and several other species of game. The rest camp at **Popa Falls** and the nearby **Mahango** are two other well-known attractions in this area.

Namibia's easternmost region, the **Caprivi**, is largely unexplored by tourists. One of the area's attractions is its prolific bird life, and nearly 70% of Namibia's bird species, many of which do not occur elsewhere, have been recorded here. Another drawcard is the rivers that can be explored by boat, and tiger fishing is popular too. **Katima Mulilo**, the main settlement, is the gateway to Victoria Falls in Zimbabwe and Chobe National Park in Botswana.

The parks and communal conservancies in the Caprivi offer visitors an opportunity to experience the wilderness atmosphere of northeastern Namibia and facilities range from very basic camp sites to community-run facilities. The camp sites are unfenced and visitors should be aware at all times of the potential danger posed by wild animals.

Northeastern Namibia is a **malaria** endemic area, and the waterways are infested with **bilharzia** (*see* page 126).

DON'T MISS

*** Popa Falls: a 1km (0.6-mile) wide series of rapids in unsurpassed surroundings.
** Mahango: prolific bird life and antelope species rarely seen elsewhere in Namibia.
** Mudumu National Park: delightful scenery and game.
** Mamili National Park: magnificent scenery and aquatic and semi-aquatic animals in the Linyanti Swamps.

Opposite: *Lianshulu Lodge guests study wildlife from a raft on the Kwando River in East Caprivi.*

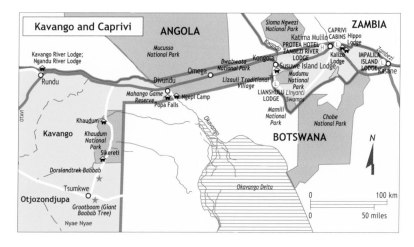

BUSHMANLAND

This region is a 1,800,000ha (4,447,893-acre) wilderness of woodlands, large baobab trees, seasonally inundated pans and open plains. Tsumkwe, administrative centre of the area, is the only large settlement; here visitors can purchase basic necessities, but no petrol is available.

The western two-thirds of the area is largely uninhabited, except for settlements at former South African Defence Force bases where !Kung San refugees from southern Angola were resettled in 1978.

Nyae Nyae (formerly known as Eastern Bushmanland) is the last stronghold of the **Ju!Wasi** who, just three decades ago, were the last of the independent hunter-gatherers in southern Africa. As a result of influences their traditional way of life collapsed permanently in the early 1970s. Today their total population in the Nyae Nyae area consists of about 3000 people living in 32 communities, and they are adapting to a new way of life.

Proclaimed in 1998 as the first communal conservancy in Namibia, the Nyae Nyae Conservancy covers some 900,000ha (2,223,900 acres) of tree savanna, woodlands and pans situated to the south and east of Tsumkwe. Enormous baobabs are a conspicuous feature of the Nyae Nyae area. Near the settlement of

TIPS FOR CAMPING IN BUSHMANLAND

• Be courteous and show respect for the Ju!Wasi culture.
• Keep to the tracks; off-road driving damages plants that the Ju!Wasi gather.
• Camping is only allowed in designated areas.
• Do not litter.
• Ensure that fires are completely burnt out.
• Ask permission to take photos of people.

Djökhoe the **Holboom** (Hollow Tree) with its hollow trunk and several other enormous baobabs growing amidst the woodlands are notable.

Game is not as abundant as in Khaudum, but during the dry season you could spot elephant, giraffe, roan antelope, warthog and wild dog, or even lion, leopard and hyena. Between December and May the seasonally inundated pans can cover up to a fifth of Nyae Nyae, attracting thousands of waterbirds. Camping is only allowed at designated camp sites. These include **Djökhoe**, lying to the southeast of Tsumkwe, and **Makuri**, which is located close to Makuri Pan, offering good birding opportunities of especially waterfowl when the pan holds water.

Except for the major gravel-surface road that leads eastwards from the B8 to Tsumkwe and the Botswana border and a few proclaimed roads in western Bushmanland, most of the roads are mere tracks. The area is accessible only by four-wheel-drive vehicle, and some tracks are impassable during the rainy season.

The turn-off to another well-known baobab, the **Dorslandboom** (Thirstland Trek Tree), is reached about 37km (23 miles) northeast of Tsumkwe on the track to Khaudum. The Thirstland Trekkers camped here in 1892 during their epic journey from the Transvaal to Angola.

Below: *A Bushman of the Nyae Nyae area near Tsumkwe. Namibia's 34,000 San people, or Bushmen, wandering hunter–gatherers by tradition, are much more sedentary than their forbears.*

KAVANGO
This region takes its name from the Kavango River, which forms Namibia's border with Angola for about 400km (248.5 miles). The river is the lifeblood of the region and nearly 75% of the people live alongside or close to it.

Khaudum National Park
North of Bushmanland is the **Khaudum National Park**, a 384,000ha

(948,884-acre) sanctuary for a variety of animals, including some 3000 elephants, roan, giraffe, eland, tsessebe, lion, wild dog and 320 bird species.

Basic camp sites are available at Sikeretti in the south and Khaudum where the hutted camps have been damaged extensively by elephants. Tourism facilities are planned for the park following the awarding of a tourism concession to the Gcuriku Traditional Authority and two communal conservancies joining the park in 2008.

Although the park has a well-developed network of tracks, the sandy terrain can only be negotiated by a four-wheel-drive vehicle. Because of the remoteness of the area, it is essential to travel in a party of at least two vehicles and to carry sufficient emergency supplies.

Rundu

Situated on the southern bank of the Kavango River, **Rundu** is the administrative centre of the Kavango region. There is little of interest to the tourist here, but the **Mbanguru Woodcarvers' Co-operative** is worth a stop on your way through the town. The Kavango people are skilled woodcarvers and items on sale range from animal carvings to wooden spoons, jewellery chests and dining-room tables and chairs. Teak is mainly used, and faces are a popular motif.

From Rundu the B2 heads in an easterly direction,

RARE ANTELOPE

Northeastern Namibia is the habitat of several semi-aquatic antelope species not found elsewhere in the country's conservation areas. **Waterbuck** can usually be seen on the floodplains and grassy areas along the rivers, while the **red lechwe** is attracted to the floodplains and shallow water. The **sitatunga** is another semi-aquatic species, but since it favours papyrus swamps it is seen only infrequently. The very rare **puku**, a species that favours dry, grassy flood-plains, used to occur in the Mamili National Park, but has become locally extinct.

Right: *Exploring the Kavango by river-boat.*

passing through dense woodlands dominated by teak trees, and reaches Divundu after about 200km (124 miles). This entire stretch is tarred.

Popa Falls ★★★

The rest camp at **Popa Falls**, a short distance beyond Divundu along the road to Botswana, is a welcome refuge on a hot day. The rustic, thatched bungalows are shaded by tall trees and the sound of the continuous gushing of the nearby cascades provides a background for the melodious calls of a rich variety of birds. There is also a grass camp site with a field kitchen and ablution facilities. As there is no restaurant, visitors must be self-sufficient. Contact Namibia Wildlife Resorts for reservations and information.

The 'falls' consists of a network of rushing channels, water courses and small islands that form a spectacular 1km (0.6-mile) wide series of rapids where the Kavango River breaks through a quartzite barrier. However, only a small section of this spectacle can be seen from the southern bank of the river. The **Popa Falls** is best viewed between July and October when the level of the river is low.

Visitors should not swim in the river because of the very real danger presented by crocodiles and hippos, and as some parts of the river are bilharzia-infested.

Mahango ★★

Mahango (formerly Mahango Game Park) has been incorporated into the Bwabwata National Park as a core conservation area. Covering 25,000ha (61,775 acres), it lies at the upper end of the Panhandle of the Okavango Delta in Botswana and comprises woodlands, floodplains and grassy, seasonally inundated river courses. The Popa Falls Rest Camp and several other establishments are close to the entrance gate which is open from sunrise to sunset. Entry permits obtainable at the gate.

There are two **circular drives** that give visitors the opportunity to explore the area. The route winding alongside the Kavango River is suitable for cars and

---

BIRDS OF NORTHEASTERN NAMIBIA

Several bird species are found only in this area or have a limited distribution elsewhere in Namibia. Species likely to be of interest to birders include the slaty egret, long-toed lapwing, African skimmer and coppery-tailed coucal. Among the noteworthy species of the riverine forest are the western banded snake eagle and Hartlaub's babbler, and the copper sunbird has been recorded at Lianshulu. The greater swamp warbler is found only in the papyrus swamps, while Bradfield's hornbill and the greater blue-eared starling can be seen in the woodlands.

CLIMATE

The climate in the northeast is subtropical. From **April** to **August** it is dry and cool with occasional **frost** and minimum temperatures of below 6°C (42.8°F). From **September** to **November** it is **hot** and **dry** with an average maximum of 35°C (95°F). The **rainy season** is from early **December** to **March/April** when 500–700mm (19.5–27.5in) of rain falls in violent **thunderstorms** and temperatures and **humidity** are unpleasantly high.

affords visitors good views of the grassy floodplains where red lechwe, reedbuck and waterbuck can be seen grazing during the early mornings. Chobe bushbuck favour the dense riverine forests, while you can look out for the elusive sitatunga in the papyrus swamps. A picnic site on the riverbank of the Kavango is a good vantage point for bird-watching.

Mahango is renowned for its large numbers of elephants, and during the dry season they are often encountered close to the river. Other animals to look out for include tsessebe, roan antelope, sable, impala and buffalo, while lion occasionally pass through the area.

The route south of the road heading to the Botswana border winds across the dunes and is negotiable by four-wheel-drive vehicle only. One of the main attractions of this area is its prolific bird life, and to date some 440 bird species have been recorded here. Since many of these are migrants, summer is the most rewarding time to visit.

Visitors may walk around in the area, but bear in mind that wild animals roam around freely, so it is not safe to venture too far from your vehicle.

WEST CAPRIVI

West Caprivi, a 32km (20-mile) wide ribbon of dense woodlands, links Kavango and East Caprivi. Known in colonial times as the Caprivi Zipfel, now often called the Caprivi Strip, this geographical curiosity stretches for 200km (124 miles) between the Kavango River in the west and the Kwando in the east. In the south it is bounded by Botswana and in the north by Angola.

Bwabwata National Park

Covering 6100km² (2355 sq miles), the Bwabwata National Park was proclaimed in 2007 when the Mahango Game Park and the Caprivi Game Park were merged, while the 20,000ha (49,420-acre) Kwando Triangle in the east was also incorporated into the new park. Mahango and Buffalo in the west and the Kwando area in the east are managed as core conservation areas. The central area of the park has been zoned as a multiple-use area for community-based tourism to enable the San to continue living in the park.

With a bird list of over 340 species and a possible 70 other species, the park is rich in bird life. Among the game to be seen are elephant, hippo, buffalo, impala, roan, sable, tsessebe, reedbuck, lion, leopard and wild dog.

Mahango, Buffalo and the Kwando core areas offer superb game-viewing, especially during the dry season when large herds of elephant congregate in these areas. Buffalo, hippo, sable, waterbuck, red lechwe, impala, lion and leopard are amongst the other species to be on the lookout for.

Tourist facilities in the west are available at **N//goabaca**, a community-run camp site. Situated on the northern bank of the Kavango River, N//goabaca overlooks Popa Falls and has four camping sites.

There are community-run camp sites at **Bum Hill**, north of the B8, and at **Nambwa**, south of the B8 in the Kwando area. Horseshoe Bend attracts large numbers of elephant in the dry season.

Below: *The enchanting malachite kingfisher, a familiar sight in the watery world of Caprivi.*

Built on a small island in the Kwando River, the **Susuwe Island Lodge** is the sister to Impalila Island Lodge, an up-market establishment offering superb service.

EAST CAPRIVI

Kongola is the gateway to **East Caprivi**, a water-rich region of floodplains bounded on all sides by rivers (the Kwando, Linyanti and Chobe), except for its northern

BEST BUYS

- **Kavango woodcarvings** from Mbanguru Co-operative in Rundu, or along the main road south of Rundu.
- **Bushman handicrafts** from San people living in Nyae Nyae.
- **Zambian and Caprivian handicrafts** such as wood and stone carvings, baskets, printed fabric and African-style clothing from the Caprivi Art Centre.
- **Caprivian handicrafts** like baskets, wood and stone carvings, and pottery from Lizauli Traditional Village.

Below: *Local art, handicrafts and African fashions are on display at the Caprivi Art Centre.*

boundary with Zambia. A 120km (75-mile) tarred road links Kongola and Katima Mulilo, but a four-wheel-drive vehicle is essential to visit the off-the-beaten-track attractions in the region.

Mudumu National Park ★★

The Kwando River with its tranquil lagoons, narrow slow-flowing channels and magnificent riverine forests forms the western boundary of this unspoilt conservation area and is an ideal habitat for hippo and crocodiles, as well as small numbers of red lechwe, reedbuck and the water-adapted sitatunga. The remainder of the 100,000ha (247,105-acre) **Mudumu National Park** is dominated by mopane woodlands where elephant, buffalo, impala, kudu, giraffe and Burchell's zebra, as well as the rare roan antelope and sable, roam. The park, which is accessible only by four-wheel-drive vehicle, is a bird-watcher's paradise and chances are that you could spot several species that do not occur elsewhere in Namibia. Look out for the distinctive African fish eagle, Pel's fishing owl and the Narina trogon. Basic facilities are available at Nakatwa. Contact the Ministry of Environment and Tourism in Katima Mulilo for permits.

Situated on the banks of the Kwando River in the Mudumu National Park, **Lianshulu Lodge** is an up-market establishment. The lodge overlooks the quiet backwaters of Lianshulu Lagoon and guests are accommodated in reed-and-thatch chales with en-suite facilities. Activities include guided walks, game-viewing drives and a sunset cruise on the Kwando River.

Accommodation is, however, available at several establishments to the north of the park. **Kubunyana**, a community-run establishment just south of Kongola, has shady camp sites on the banks of the Kwando River. There are a number of other options, including **Namushasha Lodge**, **Mazambala Island Camp** and **Kwando Camp**.

Above: *Women grinding millet at Lizauli Traditional Village.*

Visitors to the park can gain an insight into local traditions by visiting the **Lizauli Traditional Village** just outside the park boundaries. The programme is aimed at uplifting the local community and enabling them to share in the benefits of tourism.

Mamili National Park ★★

The focal point of the **Mamili National Park**, 30km (19 miles) south of Mudumu, are the **Linyanti Swamps**. When the level of the Kwando River is high, as was the case in 1978, 2008 and 2009, the floodplain grasslands are transformed into reed-lined channels, forested islands and vast reed and papyrus swamps.

More than three-quarters of the park is inaccessible when the Kwando River spills over its banks, usually in June, inundating large areas. Once the floods have subsided, however, it is possible to reach Nkasa and Lupala islands which lie at the heart of the 32,000ha (79,075-acre) park, and during the dry season Mamili is accessible by four-wheel-drive vehicle. Note that facilities are limited

---

ANGLING

The rivers of northeastern Namibia are the habitat of more than 70 species of fish and offer excellent angling opportunities. The **tiger fish** is undoubtly one of the best sporting fish in the world and trophies of over 10kg (22lb) are possible on the Zambezi River. Although fishing is possible all year round, between August and December is generally the best time to catch tiger fish. Bream, a popular eating fish, and nembwe of up to 4kg (9lb) are also caught, while barbel of up to 20kg (44lb) can be landed.

to three basic camp sites, and visitors must be totally self-sufficient, which includes bringing along your own water and firewood. Contact the Ministry of Environment and Tourism in Katima Mulilo for permits, camp site reservations and information.

Game to be seen includes large herds of elephant and buffalo, lion, leopard, spotted hyena, hippo, giraffe, impala, red lechwe, reedbuck and the elusive sitatunga. With noteworthy species such as wattled crane, rosy-throated longclaw, slaty egret, Meves' starling and greater swamp warbler, the park also offers outstanding birding.

Katima Mulilo

The administrative centre of the Caprivi region, **Katima Mulilo**, lies on the banks of the mighty Zambezi River, which forms the boundary with Zambia. The wide, slow-flowing river, fringed by tall trees, is inhabited by animals such as hippos and crocodiles, and keen birders will be quite delighted with the variety of species that can be ticked off your birding list on a short walk along the Zambezi.

The **open-air market**, where dried fish, live chickens and printed cloth are just a few of the wares traded, is worth visiting, even if only to experience the hive of

activity. Souvenir-hunters should also visit the **Caprivi Art Centre** where a selection of wood and soapstone carvings, baskets and ethnic clothing featuring lovely colourful African prints can be purchased.

Katima, is a convenient base from which to explore the waterways and game parks of East Caprivi, while the Chobe National Park in Botswana and Zimbabwe's Victoria Falls are just a few hours' drive away.

The **Protea Hotel Zambezi Lodge**, on the outskirts of the town along the banks of the Zambezi River, is known for its floating bar from where superb views can be enjoyed as you sip a sundowner. The riverine trees are rewarding for birding and you might tick green pigeon, Schalow's turaco and a variety of other species.

Accommodation is also available at **Caprivi Cabins River Lodge** and **Hippo Lodge**, both situated on the banks of the Kavango River, a few kilometres east of Katima. **Kalizo Lodge**, about 37km (23 miles) further east along the river, offers fully-inclusive fishing and canoeing safaris.

Impalila Island

Situated in the extreme northeastern corner of Namibia, Impalila Island lies where the borders of Namibia, Botswana, Angola and Zimbabwe meet. Its Silozi name appropriately means 'the far away place'. Bounded by the Zambezi River to the north and the Chobe River to the south, it is accessible only by boat or by air. **Impalila Island Lodge** offers exceptional service, a fine wilderness atmosphere and a wide range of activities including tiger fishing, mokoro trips, sundowner cruises, game-viewing from the Chobe River, guided walks on the island and outstanding birding.

Above: *Tourists negotiate the wetlands in four-wheel-drive vehicles.*
Opposite: *A dugout canoe, or mokoro, on the floodplain of the Linyanti River.*

> ### BIRDS OF EASTERN CAPRIVI
>
> With habitats ranging from woodlands to floodplain grasslands and riverine forests, more than 440 bird species, including several Okavango Delta 'specials', have been recorded in the eastern Caprivi. The region is a birder's paradise and some examples of the more noteworthy birds that have been recorded here are the slaty egret, coppery-tailed coucal, wattled crane, Pel's fishing owl, copper sunbird, southern brown-throated weaver and red-throated twinspot.

Kavango and Caprivi at a Glance

In **summer** high temperatures and humidity can be unbearable, but are tempered when rain sets in. Exploring off-the-beaten-track destinations is trying in the rainy season as large areas are flooded and tracks are muddy. Bird-watching is most rewarding during summer.

In **winter** the weather is pleasant with cool early morning and evening and pleasant daytime temperatures. The dry winter months are best for game-viewing.

Katima Mulilo is served by regular **Air Namibia** flights, tel: 061 299 6444.
There are **landing strips** near all the major lodges in the area. Other lodges will collect guests at Katima Mulilo airport by prior arrangement. For **air charter**, contact (in Windhoek) Comav, tel: 061 227 512; Desert Air, tel: 061 228 101, fax: 248 316; and Westair, tel: 061 221 091, fax: 232 778. In Swakopmund, contact Pleasure Flights, tel/fax: 064 404 500.

A four-wheel-drive vehicle is essential to explore off-the-beaten-track destinations in the Kavango and Caprivi regions, and it is also essential that you travel in a party of at least two vehicles.
Car hire is available from

Avis, tel: 067 220 824, or from Imperial-Europcar, tel: 067 220 728 in Tsumeb. Unless you have quite a large amount of time at your disposal and are very well prepared, probably the best thing to do would be to join an **organized safari** or to stay at one of the lodges in the area, all of which offer guided game-viewing drives, walks and boat trips.
A **tarred road**, approximately 700km (435 miles) long, links Windhoek and Rundu; the 520km (325-mile) **Trans-Caprivi Highway** from Rundu to Ngoma is fully tarred. The route that goes through **Bushmanland** and **Khaudum Game Park** is accessible to four-wheel-drive vehicles only. The Namibia/Botswana **border posts** Mohembo and Ngoma, as well as the Namibia/Zambia border post Wenela, are open every day, 06:00 to 18:00.

Kavango
Sarasungu River Lodge, located 4km (2.5 miles) to the northeast of Rundu on banks of the Kavango River. Offers its visitors comfortable reed-and-thatch bungalows, an à la carte restaurant, bar and a swimming pool. Various activities, including canoeing trips and good birding opportunities are available for guests, tel: 066 255 161.
Kavango River Lodge, Rundu:

self-catering accommodation with views over the Kavango River, tel and fax: 066 255 244.
Ngandu Safari Lodge, Rundu, overlooking the Kavango River: accommodation ranges from luxury en-suite units to self-catering facilities, tel: 066 256 723, fax: 256 726.
Ngepi Camp, overlooking the Kavango River, downstream of Popa Falls; offers camp sites, tree houses, bush huts, restaurant, bar, viewing deck and a variety of activities; close to Mahango, tel: 066 259 903, fax: 259 906.

Caprivi
Caprivi River Lodge, 5km (3 miles) from Katima Mulilo: on banks of Zambezi River; offers thatched bungalows with en-suite facilities, tel: 066 252 288.
Hippo Lodge, 6km (4 miles) east of Katima Mulilo: on the Zambezi River; has brick-and-reed huts with en-suite facilities, a camp site, an open-air à la carte restaurant, a bar, and a swimming pool, tel/fax: 066 253 684.
Lianshulu Lodge, Mudumu National Park: overlooks Lianshulu Lagoon on the Kwando River and has rustic reed-and-wood chalets with en-suite facilities; there is also a dining area, lounge and bar, tel: 061 274 545.
Impalila Island Lodge, on Impalila Island in extreme east of Namibia: on Zambezi

River; wood chalets with en-suite facilities, swimming pool; fishing, birding, boat trips, game-viewing, tel/fax: +27 11 234 9997.

Susuwe Island Lodge, on a small island in the Kwando River: luxury accommodation in thatched chalets with en-suite facilities, wooden deck, plunge pool, nature walks, game drives, boat trips, good birding, tel: +27 11 234 9997.

Protea Hotel Zambezi River Lodge, in Katima Mulilo: offers accommodation on the banks of the Zambezi River in comfortable en-suite rooms, also camp sites, restaurant, floating bar, swimming pool, nine-hole golf course, gym and sauna, tel: 066 251 500, fax: 253 631.

Restaurants and various accommodation establish-ments in Rundu and Katima Mulilo serve meals.

Kalizo Lodge offers fishing on the Zambezi River, boating, birding and trips to Victoria Falls and other destinations, tel: 066 686 802.

Lianshulu Lodge offers nature drives, walks, night drives, boat trips on the Kwando and bird-watching, tel: 061 274 545.

Impalila Island Lodge offers fishing, excellent birding, walks, boat trips and game-viewing, tel: +27 11

234 9997.

Ngepi Camp, offers canoe trips, sunset cruises and fishing on the Kavango River, guided walks and visits to local villages, tel: 066 259 903, fax: 259 906.

Self-drive tours of Caprivi and the Kavango are organized by Ondese Travel and Safaris, PO Box 6196, Ausspannplatz, Windhoek, tel: 061 220 876, fax: 239 700; a **fly-in safari** to Caprivi is offered by Namib Travel Shop, tel: 061 226 174, fax: 239 455; Sense of Africa, tel: 061 275 300, also offers a **four-wheel-drive tour** of Caprivi that includes the Chobe National Park in Botswana and the Victoria Falls in Zimbabwe; SWA Safaris, tel: 061 221 193, fax: 225 387, operates **safari tours** of Caprivi and Botswana that include a day excursion to the Victoria Falls in Zimbabwe. Before you venture off to explore off-the-beaten-track destinations make sure that you are well equipped and prepared: contact the Surveyor-General, situated on the corner of Robert Mugabe Avenue and Dr AB May

Street, Windhoek, tel: 061 245 056, fax: 249 802, for **topographical maps**; the **Automobile Association** (AA), located on the corner of Independence Avenue and Fidel Castro Street, tel: 061 224 201, fax: 222 446, pro-vides members with useful travel information; Camping Hire Namibia in Windhoek, tel: 061 252 995, has a wide range of **camping equipment** for hire.

Birds of the Eastern Caprivi by J. H. Koen.
Bushmen: A Changing Way of Life by Anthony Bannister and David Lewis-Williams.
Popular Checklist of the Birds of South West Africa/Namibia by A. J. Williams.
Sasol Birds of Southern Africa by Ian Sinclair.

Ministry of Environment and Tourism, Katima Mulilo, tel: 066 253 027.
Namibia Wildlife Resorts, Windhoek, tel: 061 285 7200 for reservations and information.

RUNDU	J	F	M	A	M	J	J	A	S	O	N	D
AVERAGE TEMP. °F	77	75	75	73	66	61	61	66	73	79	79	77
AVERAGE TEMP. °C	25	24	24	23	19	16	16	19	23	26	26	25
RAINFALL in	6	6	3.5	1.5	0.5	0	0	0	0	1	2	3.5
RAINFALL mm	146	148	87	38	12	0	0	0	2	20	58	85
DAYS OF RAINFALL	16	16	12	6	2	0	0	0	1	5	9	12
HUMIDITY	68	72	69	62	53	50	46	39	33	38	53	61

Travel Tips

Tourist Information

Namibia Tourism has offices in South Africa (Johannesburg and Cape Town), the United Kingdom (London) and Germany (Frankfurt).
The Namibia Tourism Board's office in Windhoek is on the ground floor of the Sanlam Centre, corner of Fidel Castro and Werner List streets, tel: 061 290 6000, fax: 254848. e-mail: info@ namibiatourism.com.na

Regional tourism and publicity associations are represented in a number of towns: **Windhoek Information and Publicity**, tel: 061 290 2092; **Southern Tourist Forum**, tel: 063 221 266; **Lüderitz Information Bureau**, tel: 063 202 532; **Tsumeb Tourism Centre**, tel: 067 220 728; **Namib-i** in Swakopmund, tel: 064 404 827 and **Rundu Tourism Centre**, tel: 066 256 140.

Reservations for state-owned accommodation in game parks and resorts are handled by the central reservations office of **Namibia Wildlife Resorts** in Erkrath Building, 189 Independence Avenue, Windhoek. Written applications must be directed to Reservations, Private Bag 13267, Windhoek, tel: 061 285 7200. Namibia Wildlife Resorts also has an office in Swakopmund, tel: 064 402 172.

Entry Requirements

All visitors must have a valid passport, and temporary residence permits for visitors are issued on arrival and allow tourists a period of 90 days in the country. Bona fide tourists and business travellers of these countries are exempted from visa requirements: Angola, Australia, Austria, Belgium, Botswana, Brazil, Canada, Cuba, Denmark, France, Germany, Iceland, Ireland, Italy, Japan, Kenya, Lesotho, Lichtenstein, Luxembourg, Malawi, Malaysia, Mozambique, Netherlands, New Zealand, Norway, Portugal, Russia, Singapore, South Africa, Spain, Swaziland, Switzerland, Tanzania, United Kingdom, United States of America, Zambia, Zimbabwe. Visitors are, however, advised to confirm visa requirements with their travel agent.

Health Requirements

Vaccinations against smallpox, cholera and yellow fever are not required. However, visitors travelling from or through countries where yellow fever is endemic must have a valid International Certificate of Vaccination. This requirement does not apply to air travellers in transit. No AIDS screening tests are conducted.

Air Travel

Hosea Kutako International Airport, 45km (28 miles) west of the capital, is the major point of entry into Namibia (see page 42). Eros Airport, 4km (2.5 miles) from the city centre, is served by domestic flights. Air Namibia, the national carrier, has regular scheduled flights to Katima Mulilo, Lüderitz, Ondangwa, Oranjemund, and Walvis Bay. There are landing strips throughout the country and air-charter services are available in Windhoek, Swakopmund and Walvis Bay (see page 42).

Road Travel

Namibia has a well-developed road system, covering some 40,000km (24,856 miles). Trunk roads covering 5000km (3107 miles) are tarred and connect all the main centres, while major gravel-surface roads are generally in a good condition. The state of district and farm roads varies from good to poor, depending on when they were last graded. Motoring tips: During the summer months care should be exercised on gravel-surface roads as washaways are common after rains. Motorists should look out for wild or domestic animals as they can cause serious accidents. Warthogs feed in the long grass alongside the road and are in the habit of suddenly crossing it. Kudu are a danger at night in densely vegetated areas, and warning signs should be heeded. In rural areas, domestic animals are not fenced so be careful. Always carry emergency spares and sufficient water (at least 10 litres; 2.6 gallons) with you, especially on the lonely back roads.

Driver's licence: The carrying of driver's licences is compulsory. Foreign licences are acceptable if they carry a photograph and are either printed in English or accompanied by an English-language certificate of authenticity. An alternative is to obtain an International Driving Permit before departing for Namibia. Licences issued in Botswana, Lesotho, South Africa, Swaziland and Zimbabwe are valid in Namibia.

Road rules and signs: In Namibia one drives on the left-hand side of the road. Speed limits are 120kph (75mph) on major roads and 60kph (37mph) in urban areas, unless otherwise indicated. Depending on the condition of gravel-surface roads, the recommended speed is between 80kph (50mph) and 100kph (62mph). All proclaimed routes are numbered (major routes with the prefix B, secondary routes with prefix C, district roads with prefix D and farm roads with prefix P or F), and tourist attractions are generally well marked.

Car hire: Avis, Budget Europcar, Hertz and Imperial are represented in Windhoek and have branches in most major towns throughout the country. Several companies specialize in four-wheel-drive vehicles, and Britz: Namibia rents out campervans. Telephone numbers are given in the At a Glance section of each chapter.

Insurance: Third-party insurance is included in the price of fuel. The excess for damage to hired vehicles is high as most driving is on gravel roads with high accident rates. When making reservations, establish the excess and the renter's responsibility in respect of collision damage waiver insurance. Maps: The road map published by the AA of Namibia is useful, and there are several commercially published maps of the country. The *Globetrotter Travel Map of Namibia* is excellent, as is the *MapStudio Touring Atlas of Namibia*.

Petrol: Petrol is available at filling stations throughout Namibia. In Windhoek and some of the larger towns fuel is available 24 hours a day, but in some of the smaller towns and settlements pumps close at 18:00, while restricted hours could apply during weekends. The availability of fuel at some settlements in remote areas is unreliable at times and you should ensure that you have sufficient fuel to get to your destination. In the northwest of Namibia petrol is available only at Ruacana, Sesfontein and Opuwo. Cash only is accepted for petrol in rural areas.

Automobile Association of Namibia: The AAN office is in the Carl List Building, on the corner of Independence Avenue and Fidel Castro Street, tel: 061 224 201. The AA has tow-in service contractors in all major towns. The after-hours breakdown number is: 061 224 201. Maps of Namibia and other southern African countries are also available.

Coach travel: Intercape Mainliner operates a luxury coach service between Windhoek and Walvis Bay, and between Windhoek and Victoria Falls. There are also regular coach departures from the capital to Cape Town and Johannesburg in South Africa.

What to Wear

During the day dress is usually casual, but in some of the more sophisticated hotel restaurants and bars, jeans, T-shirts and slip-slops are not acceptable in the evening when 'smart casual' clothes are the norm.

Early mornings and evenings can be cold during winter (May to September), so pack warm clothing such as trousers, long-sleeved shirts, a jersey or anorak. During the hot summer months (October to April) loose-fitting clothes, a wide-rimmed hat and a raincoat are essential. After rain, temperatures drop by quite a few degrees so include a light jersey for the occasional cool summer evening. Mosquitoes can be troublesome during summer, so remember to pack loose-fitting trousers and long-sleeved shirts to protect legs and arms during the evenings. Warm clothing is necessary throughout the year along the coast where fog and a chilly breeze can create unpleasant conditions.

Money Matters

The Namibian currency unit is the Namibia dollar (N$), divided into 100 cents. Coins are issued in denominations of 5c, 10c, 50c, $1 and $5; notes in denominations of $10, $50 and $100. The Namibia dollar has the same value as the South African rand, which is still legal tender in Namibia.

Currency exchange: Foreign currency can be converted into Namibia dollars at banks and bureaux de change in Windhoek. No foreign currencies are accepted at state-owned rest camps, nor are facilities to exchange foreign currency available. Hosea Kutako International Airport has currency-exchange

facilities. Namibian currency should be converted to foreign currency before leaving the country.

Banks: First National Bank and Standard Bank are represented throughout Namibia. Banking hours are from 09:00 to 15:30 on weekdays and 08:30 to 11:00 on Saturdays, except in country towns where banks close between 13:00 and 14:00.

Travellers' cheques: may be cashed at any bank and at major hotels in Windhoek. State-owned rest camps and resorts will only cash travellers' cheques in South African rand.

Credit cards: Most hotels, restaurants, shops, car-hire firms and tour operators accept international credit cards (American Express, Visa, Diners Club and MasterCard). Some German-owned businesses, guest farms in remote areas and shops in rural areas do not accept credit cards. Petrol cannot be bought with a credit card; some banks, however, issue a special

'Petrocard' or 'Autocard'.

Value Added Tax: VAT of 15 per cent is payable on most goods and services, but visitors may claim VAT refunds.

Tipping: It is customary to tip porters, waiters, waitresses, taxi drivers, room attendants and golf caddies, provided the service is satisfactory. It is usual to tip petrol attendants about N$2 when they offer to clean car windows or to check the water, oil and tyre pressure. Gratuities for waiters/waitresses and taxi drivers are usually 10 per cent of the bill, and tips for porterage are around N$2 per bag.

Accommodation

All accommodation establishments in Namibia, including hotels, pensions (private hotels), guest farms, rest camps and caravan parks, are graded. All accommodation establishments in Namibia must be registered with the Namibia Tourism Board to ensure that high standards are maintained. Provision is made for registration in 13 categories ranging from backpackers hostels, bed-and-

CONVERSION CHART		
FROM	**TO**	**MULTIPLY BY**
Millimetres	Inches	0.0394
Metres	Yards	1.0936
Metres	Feet	3.281
Kilometres	Miles	0.6214
Hectares	Acres	2.471
Litres	Pints	1.760
Kilograms	Pounds	2.205
Tonnes	Tons	0.984
To convert Celsius to Fahrenheit: x 9 ÷ 5 + 32		

breakfasts, guest houses and camp sites to hotels, guest farms and lodges. There is also an increasing number of self-catering facilities.

Hotel pensions must have at least 10, but not more than 20 rooms and must serve breakfast. Accommodation in rest camps is provided in rooms, rondavels, bungalows or other accommodation units and may also include camping sites. Guest farms are known for their typical Namibian hospitality and offer guests an opportunity to experience farm life and to participate in farming activities. Lodges are located in rural areas or within a natural environment and must provide recreational facilities such as game drives, a health spa or other activities. Namib Sun Hotels, Namibia Country Lodges, United Africa Hospitality, Wilderness Safaris and Leading Lodges of Africa have establishments throughout the country. Most lodges, permanent tented camps and tented lodges cater for the luxury market.

Rest camps and resorts: Rest camps and resorts in state-owned conservation areas are run by Namibia Wildlife Resorts, a commercial public company, tel: 061 285 7200 for reservations and information. Accommodation ranging from modern bungalows to rustic thatched huts is provided in nearly all state-owned game parks, reserves and resorts, and camp sites with facilities are provided in rest camps, except at Terrace Bay.

Bedding and towels are provided at all the rest camps (except Von Bach Dam Resort and Khaudum Game Park) but no crockery, cutlery or cooking utensils. The major rest camps and resorts all have à la carte restaurants serving breakfast, lunch and dinner.

PUBLIC HOLIDAYS

New Year's Day (1 January)
Independence Day (21 March)
Good Friday
Easter Monday
Workers' Day (1 May)
Cassinga Day (4 May)
Ascension Day
Africa Day (25 May)
Heroes' Day (26 August)
Human Rights Day (10 December)
Christmas Day (25 December)
Family Day (26 December)

Trading Hours

Normal business hours are from 08:00 or 08:30 to 17:00 or 17:30 Mondays to Fridays and 08:00 to 13:00 on Saturdays. Shops are closed on Sundays and public holidays, but most supermarkets have restricted trading hours on Sundays and public holidays.

Measurements

Namibia, like the rest of southern Africa, uses the metric system.

Telephones

Namibia's country dialling code for overseas callers is 264. The telecommunications system in the major towns is fully automated and calls can be made to over 200 countries. Dialling inside Namibia is fully automated except to a few remote settlements. Dialling codes, telephone numbers, fax numbers and telex numbers are listed in one directory, available at any post office, for the entire country. Public coin and card phones are available throughout the country.

Enquiries: For numbers that have changed or are not listed in the telephone directory, dial 1188.

Time

In summer, Namibian Standard Time is two hours ahead of Greenwich Mean Time and the same as South African Standard Time; in winter, Namibian Standard Time is one hour ahead of Greenwich Mean Time and thus one hour behind South African Standard Time. Summer time commences at 02:00 on the first Sunday of September; winter time commences at 02:00 on the first Sunday of April.

Electricity

Electrical appliances operate on 220/240 volts. Plugs are 3-pin (round), 15 amp. Not all electric shavers will fit hotel and game-park plug points, and visitors are advised to seek advice from a local electrical supplier.

Medical Services

It is advisable to take out medical insurance before your departure for Namibia.

Hospitals: Windhoek has three private hospitals, the Roman Catholic Hospital in Werner List Street, Medi-Clinic in Erospark and the Rhino Park Private Hospital. There is a Medi-Clinic in Otjiwarongo, and Swakopmund has the Cottage Private Hospital. In Walvis Bay is the Welwitschia Hospital. Tsumeb also has a private hospital. Some churches in the north of the country run hospitals or clinics, and there are state hospitals in major towns. Emergency evacuation is expensive and visitors should ensure that they have adequate insurance, including emergency evacuation.

Doctors: Medical practitioners are listed in the orange pages in the telephone directory.

Pharmacies: All major towns have pharmacies, usually open during normal business hours; some pharmacies in Windhoek have extended trading hours. In rural areas medication is often available only from the state hospital or clinic.

Health Hazards

Malaria: Malaria is endemic in the east, north and north-east of the country and it is important to take precautions throughout the year. The disease is epidemic from the Etosha Pan westwards and in the northern parts of Kaokoland, occurring in particular during the rainy season. As the recommended anti-malarial drugs could change from time to time, it is important to consult your doctor or a pharmacist well in advance. It is equally important to take

the tablets as prescribed and to continue taking the tablets for the advised period after leaving the malaria area.

Bilharzia: This waterborne parasite attacks the bladder, intestines and other organs of humans, livestock and game. It is found in still water (like dams), stagnant water (like pools) and slow-moving water in some parts of rivers. So, avoid swimming, drinking or washing in dams and rivers.

AIDS: Considering the size of Namibia's population, the number of HIV positive cases is relatively high. However, if the necessary precautions are taken, visitors need not fear contracting the disease. All blood is screened for hepatitis and AIDS by the Blood Transfusion Service of Namibia. The blood is tested by qualified staff according to standard, internationally recognized methods, and is regularly submitted to strict quality controls.

Creepy crawlies: A wide variety of snakes, scorpions, spiders and stinging insects occur in Namibia, but most bites and stings will only cause discomfort. The chances of being bitten or stung are most likely when you are camping out in the open or undertaking walks and trails, and can be minimized by taking a few simple precautions.

Avoid scorpion bites by shaking out your shoes or boots before putting them on in the morning, and do not walk around barefoot or without a torch at night. Ticks are mainly encountered in grassy

areas but being bitten does not mean that you will get tick-bite fever. The possibility of tick bites can be reduced by wearing long trousers and by inspecting your clothes and body thoroughly during rest stops and at the end of the day. Remove ticks as soon as possible after they are detected by pulling them away from the body or covering them with a greasy substance.

Emergencies

The national emergency number for the Police is 10111, while the numbers of ambulance services in major towns are listed in the telephone directory on the page preceding subscribers' numbers in the particular town. The two personal crisis help services in Windhoek, Alcoholics Anonymous and Lifeline, are also listed in the telephone directory.

Security

As a rule it is quite safe to walk around the streets of Windhoek and other towns after dark without fear of being attacked, although isolated incidents do occur from time to time so some basic precautions are advisable. Avoid looking like the typical tourist, do not carry large amounts of cash on your person and hand valuables in for safekeeping at hotels. In some rural areas petty thieving has become a problem, so do not leave camping gear and other valuables unattended; rather lock them away.

INDEX